Way Outback

by Bill Rosoman Dip CS

Copies of this ebook can be ordered from
www.smashwords.com/profile/view/leftfieldnz
http://stores.lulu.com/leftfieldnz

ISBN 978-1-927157-20-6

Table of Contents

Preface

This is my online business card. Just scan with your smart phone or computer to see the card.

http://www.creativekiwis.com/
www.smashwords.com/profile/view/leftfieldnz
http://stores.lulu.com/leftfieldnz

Pictures at
http://goo.gl/XmvGZ

Videos at
www.youtube.com/leftfieldnz

My Blog is at
Www.leftfieldnz.blog.com

I am a Baby Boomer (born 1948), I am 63 in 2011. I have been chugging along in life but trying to improve my lot as best I can.

I worked as a Public Servant from 1965 to 1988 (New Zealand Post Office then Telecom when Privatised, as a Lineman, installing/fixing Telephones).

Up until 1984 New Zealand had a closed economy with import tariffs, price controls, a fixed currency and large subsidies for farmers etc. mostly under Prime Minister Muldoon. We were living in lala land and going broke.

Rogernomics was a complete change to a modern economy were a lot of Government Enterprises were flogged off to private enterprise and the exchange rate was floated under the Lange Labour Government.

I always say that we needed to change but it is the way they went about it and the speed of change. All the workers got screwed and the rich got much richer.

We were told to accept the pain as there would some gain done the track. Well 25 years on I am still feeling the pain.

I have lived a pretty simple non-extravagant lifestyle and have not gambled much, taken drugs or drunk much, but the money has just disappeared!

I sold my house in Tokomaru Bay on the East Coast in 1999 as there was just no employment. I moved to Gisborne and had some employment there but that dried up in 2002. I then moved to Hamilton and in the last 10 years have had some employment but have also had long periods of unemployment. I did spend a year and got my Diploma in Computing (not that it has helped in the way of employment).

At this time (September 2011) I am working 12 hour night shifts as a security guard on a bridge building site on the minimum wage of $13 an hour.

I am also concerned about the current World Economic melt down (see next Chapter)

I started looking around for property in the region of Huntly in the Waikato were I have been living on and off for the last few years.

BTW I should mention I live in a Mobile Home (RV).

Anyway all the above led me to buy a section in Glen Afton which is 15 minutes from Huntly, which is 30 minutes from Hamilton City.

Partly I have brought the section to hunker down if I loose my job and or the world economic crisis is going to bite harder.

So this book is about my adventure at going bush or frugal living or fringe dweller or survivalist or prepper or off-grid or homesteader or downsizer or when the SHTF.

Disclaimer

This book is not anti American, it is anti greed, anti multinational corporations, anti banksters.

Mind you I am reminded of Churchill, who said, "the Americans always do the right thing, when they have tried everything else".

I think all western countries and the OECD, World Bank, IMF, the Fed Reserve all need to kick in the pants and need to rain in the banking and corporate thieves.

It is time for a sea change in the way we do business, the way we share resources and look after the poor and vulnerable.

The Status Quo is not an Option.

It is time for a change.

As mentioned in this book, one Ron Paul is standing for the Republicans as a potential US President http://www.ronpaul2012.com/the-issues/ron-paul-plan-to-restore-america/

SYNOPSIS:
America is the greatest nation in human history. Our respect for individual liberty, free markets, and limited constitutional government produced the strongest, most prosperous country in the world. But, we have drifted far from our founding principles, and America is in crisis. Ron Paul's "Restore America" plan slams on the brakes and puts America on a return to constitutional government. It is bold but achievable. Through the bully pulpit of the presidency, the power of the Veto, and, most importantly, the united voice of freedom-loving Americans, we can implement fundamental reforms.

SPENDING:

Cuts $1 trillion in spending during the first year of Ron Paul's presidency, eliminating five cabinet departments (Energy, HUD, Commerce, Interior, and Education), abolishing the Transportation Security Administration and returning responsibility for security to private property owners, abolishing corporate subsidies, stopping foreign aid, ending foreign wars, and returning most other spending to 2006 levels.

But he wants to severely curtail government spending and business restraints and we would be left with economic and social anarchy.

He also wants to completely abandon foreign policy and foreign aid.

Sometimes I think some Americans are a bit deluded and are very slow learners.

Mission on, TSHTF

Well after months of preparing and writing this book finally TSHTF.

It was not as I had expected but still it was going to happen. For the first time in my life I got fired from my Security Guard job.

I made a small error of judgement and paid a large price. It could have been handled very differently by the company, but that's life.

I had been working extra time of a few weeks, so one morning I decided to leave early from my job at a mined shaft drilling site. That started a whole chain of events that I had not expected.

I thought if I got caught I would get told off and warned but not sacked. They are an areshole company, they are part of Tyco International, a very mean company.

The job I was doing was going to run out in mid-January 2012 anyway, so it is no great loss.

But you know how bad luck runs in threes!

Well in the past week, I have been fired and lost my job, I finally went to an optician with my worsening eyesight and was told I have cataracts, if I am lucky I will get on the public hospital waiting list, wait six months or more and then maybe get one eye fixed for free. The third disaster was a large truck clipping my parked van in a compound were I was picking up some of my stuff to move to my new place. The damage was not too much just another pain in life.

Oh well, "today is beginning of the rest of my life".

Now it is time to practice what I preached in this book, LOL.

I am fairly well prepared and have most things I need for now.

I sold my old large mobile home for $9,000,I have paid off my credit card and have ordered a solar panel and regulator and will have a large tree felled on my property.

That will set me up for the next year or two till I see which way the wind blows.

I have a meeting to see if I can get a benefit, probably a sickness benefit to see me through till I retire on nation superannuation at 65 in eighteen months time. Then I will get $350 per week and a few other perks and that will be plenty for me.

Reminds me of my Dad who died a year ago, he t=retired at 62 and died at 97, a long retirement. He lost his driver licence at 93 when he ran a red light and hit a ladies car side on. A pretty good innings.

So I am sitting at my new outdoor table I built recently, planning the rest of my life.

I need to get this book finished and up online. and then get stuck into my other crafts.

I have plenty of food and am eating produce from my

garden. I go to town 14km away now and then for food, water and to empty my porta-potti.

It is summer and life is great!

Kia Kaha, Be Strong, Every day is a good day,

World Financial Meltdown

At the present time (2011) we are in the middle of a an Economic Meltdown, which they say will probably get worse and taken one to two decades to ride out. The so called GFC, Global Financial Crisis.

Late-2000s financial crisis
From Wikipedia, the free encyclopedia

The late-2000s financial crisis (often called the Credit Crunch or the Global Financial Crisis) is considered by many economists to be the worst financial crisis since the Great Depression of the 1930s.[1] It was triggered by a liquidity shortfall in the United States banking system[2] and has resulted in the collapse of large financial institutions, the bailout of banks by national governments, and downturns in stock markets around the world. In many areas, the housing market has also suffered, resulting in numerous evictions, foreclosures and prolonged vacancies. It contributed to the failure of key businesses, declines in consumer wealth estimated in the trillions of U.S. dollars, and a significant decline in economic activity, leading to a severe global economic recession in 2008.[3]

The collapse of the U.S. housing bubble, which peaked in 2006, caused the values of securities tied to U.S. real estate pricing to plummet, damaging financial institutions globally.[4] Questions regarding bank solvency, declines in credit availability and damaged investor confidence had an impact on global stock markets, where securities suffered large losses during 2008 and early 2009. Economies worldwide slowed during this period, as credit tightened and international trade declined.[5] Critics argued that credit rating agencies and investors failed to accurately price the risk involved with mortgage-related financial products, and that governments did not adjust their regulatory practices to address 21st-century financial markets.[6] Governments and central banks responded with unprecedented fiscal stimulus, monetary policy expansion and institutional bailouts.

On Radio New Zealand National they have just had a three part series from the BBC on the Commodity Bubble that is looming.

Are we headed for a crash in commodities like the one in 1987 in equities? I doubt it. But, I am concerned that the commodities bubble is getting well out of hand. Certainly, the rationale for commodities as an inflation hedge and in a world of scarce resources is well-founded. However, the rise of late is downright frightening.

Soros says commodity bubble echoes '87 climate
George Soros agrees. He went before the U.S. senate and testified that he believes the commodities bubble has hallmarks of 1987 written all over it. Now, that's frightening.

MarketWatch has an article prefaced with this summary:
The investment flood into commodity indexes bears eerie similarities to the craze for portfolio insurance that led to the stock-market crash of 1987, according to hedge-fund investor George Soros, who warned that the rush into oil has created a "bubble."

Later the article spells it out. Financial institutions like mutual and hedge funds are going crazy: Lured by cheaper prices in longer-dated futures contracts, financial institutions continued to pile into the asset class as that initial opportunity disappeared. That's because commodities turned out to be more profitable than other assets -- a "classic case of misconception that is liable to be self-reinforcing in both directions," he commented.
-MarketWatch, 3 June 2008
Stay tuned. This is a story whose ending you will be interested in.

http://www.stuff.co.nz/business/world/5120593/US-debt-default-seen-as-big-global-risk
Forget reverberations of Japan's quake, high oil prices and Europe's debt crisis. The biggest risk to the world economy currently is the US government defaulting on its debt.

At least that's how St Louis Federal Reserve Bank President James Bullard sees it.

"The US fiscal situation, if not handled correctly, could turn into a global macro shock," Bullard said in an interview on Wednesday. "The idea that the US could threaten to default is a dangerous one."

It's a hotly debated issue: Some Republican lawmakers think a brief US default is acceptable if it forces the White House to deal with large budget deficits. Few Wall Street analysts believe it will come to that.

Bullard worries about reaction overseas if the US government would technically default -- basically delaying interest payments for a couple of days. That could happen in the absence of a political compromise on this year's budget.

"If it were just US markets, it might not cause too many problems, but we've got people participating in foreign markets who are probably not as tuned in to the US political situation," Bullard said. "The reverberations in those global markets would be very severe. That's where the real risk comes in."

US Debt Clock.org		
State Debt Clocks	World Debt Clocks	Debt Clock Time Machine

US PUBLIC DEBT SUBJECT TO LIMIT
$14,286,251,492,604

US NATIONAL DEBT	DEBT PER CITIZEN	DEBT PER TAXPAYER
$14,429,979,650,958	$46,315	$129,332

US FEDERAL TAX REVENUE	INCOME TAX	PAYROLL TAX	CORPORATE TAX
$2,192,048,490,349	$939,519,926,921	$844,057,114,985	$195,552,801,397

US FEDERAL SPENDING	US FEDERAL BUDGET DEFICIT
$3,570,730,592,978	$1,378,682,109,462

STATE REVENUE	STATE DEBT	LOCAL REVENUE	LOCAL DEBT
$1,179,560,128,913	$1,188,523,999,082	$1,134,868,043,767	$1,734,023,199,213

Largest Budget Items

MEDICARE/MEDICAID	SOCIAL SECURITY	DEFENSE/WARS
$817,129,845,495	$712,837,280,193	$699,471,444,266

INCOME SECURITY	NET INTEREST ON DEBT	FEDERAL PENSIONS
$424,796,868,869	$209,747,837,406	$209,292,560,472

US GROSS DOMESTIC PRODUCT	TOTAL FEDERAL/STATE/LOCAL SPENDING
$14,750,200,937,992	$6,873,818,242,146

GROSS DEBT TO GDP RATIO	REVENUE TO GDP RATIO	SPENDING TO GDP RATIO
97.8293686 %	30.5519900 %	46.6013149 %

US POPULATION	311,558,054
US INCOME TAXPAYERS	111,564,097
OFFICIAL UNEMPLOYED	13,895,130
ACTUAL UNEMPLOYED	24,262,718
STATE/LOCAL EMPLOYEES	15,943,862
FEDERAL EMPLOYEES	4,302,343
US WORK FORCE	139,790,691
US RETIREES & SSI	65,452,001
US FAMILIES	82,017,403
FOOD STAMP RECIPIENTS	45,014,506
BANKRUPTCIES · 2011	1,601,014

US TOTAL INTEREST · 2011	INTEREST PER CITIZEN	US TOTAL DEBT	TOTAL DEBT PER CITIZEN	TOTAL DEBT PER FAMILY	SAVINGS PER FAMILY
$3,613,033,273,378	$11,596	$54,970,102,389,977	$176,437	$670,235	$7,042

TOTAL PERSONAL DEBT	MORTGAGE DEBT	CONSUMER DEBT	CREDIT CARD DEBT	PERSONAL DEBT PER CIT.
$16,086,123,423,293	$13,242,659,859,145	$2,437,888,474,616	$788,562,147,139	$51,632

Money Creation

FEDERAL RESERVE MONETARY BASE	M2 MONEY SUPPLY	TREASURY SECURITIES	CURRENCY AND CREDIT DERIVATIVES
$2,663,271,896,648	$9,116,405,447,032	$1,414,993,175,230	$609,419,867,736,058

Trade Numbers

US DEBT HELD BY FOREIGN COUNTRIES	US TRADE DEFICIT	US TRADE DEFICIT · CHINA	US IMPORTED OIL	IMPORTED OIL · OPEC
$4,548,927,892,911	$693,773,525,801	$349,660,013,100	$440,546,700,967	$182,741,211,899

SMALL BUSINESS ASSETS	CORPORATION ASSETS	HOUSEHOLD ASSETS	TOTAL NATIONAL ASSETS	ASSETS PER CITIZEN
$4,547,980,078,819	$13,217,363,284,670	$57,620,870,258,838	$75,386,213,375,853	$241,979

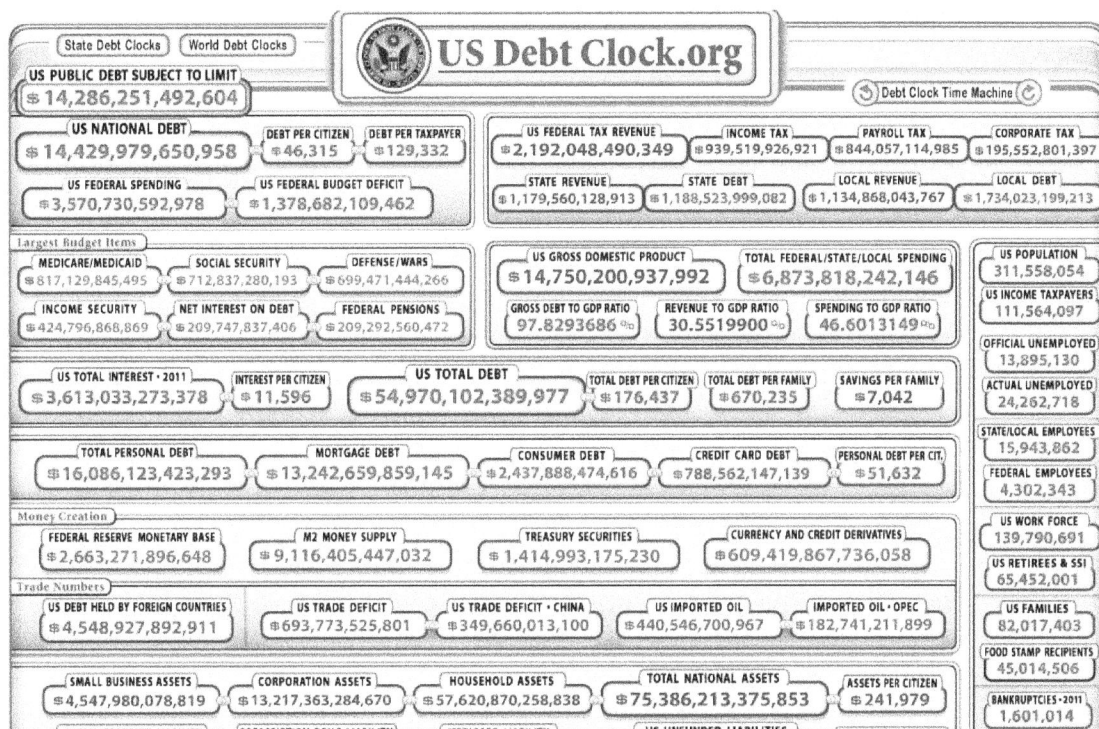

http://www.usdebtclock.org/

The USA debt is now $US15 Trillion and there are 24 million unemployed.

As a guy said on the radio today (about current politics) if you are not scared about some of this stuff you are not paying attention.

It is becoming like a perfect storm with a batch of economic disasters all coming together.

So with these batch of problems, my own job insecurity and my lack of cash I have taken the plunge and brought a cheap section and am going bush way out back.

These world banksters just can not be trusted.

I read today that there are 39 million Americans living in poverty. That is a sad fact and means 10% of the US population is living in poverty.
Source Reuters.

http://www.john-f-kennedy.net/thefederalreserve.htm
This was on the JFK website, they were talking about the US Federal Reserve and what it gets up to and how it is a Private Company and not part of the US Government. JFK signed an order

to bypass the FED but was assassinated several months later.

The following is a list of 10 things that you can do if you really want life and liberty:

1.Inform yourself. You have already taken the first an most important step, now don't stop. Do research on your own and watch videos. You can be consummately filled with information. Also, read, understand, and KNOW YOU RIGHTS – before you lose them. First, I suggest you get a copy of the Bill of Rights and memorize them and then the Constitution. If you don't know your rights, then you do not have any. The people taking them away from you or who are ignoring and/or attacking them are not going to let you know what they are.

2.Once you have your positions and ideas (whatever they may be) formed firmly in your mind and can explain how all of this is connected, then use this information to educate others. Use informational sources to help convince them. Try to avoid telling people exactly what to do, they will find their own path.

3.If you can, move out of the larger cities. We are much easier to control and/or exterminated if we are gathered in the big cities and they are implementing devious and incremental ways to herd us into them.

4.Invest as much as you can afford (preferably in this order) in water, food, weapons, survival tools, and gold/silver/copper/palladium/platinum/rhodium. Pre-1964 U.S. Dimes, quarters, halves, and silver dollars contain 90% silver. Also, pre-1982 pennies contain the most copper. Knowledge of self-defence wouldn't be a bad thing to invest in either.

5.Make amends with friends and family. Stick together and spread out throughout the U.S. in lesser populated areas in smallish groups.

6.Vote conscientiously. I will not tell you how to vote. What I will say is that if Ron Paul is not elected the next president then I, personally, will certainly step-up my preparations for a coming apocalypse.

7.When you recognize an instance where you know your rights and liberties are being taken away, attacked or challenged, stand against the opposition and say ”NO! I KNOW MY RIGHTS!” and seek help and/or legal representation and do your best to expose and publicize it.

8.Whenever you have the privilege of speaking with an armed official (Army, Navy, Air Force, Marine, ROTC, National Guard, policeman, FBI, Border Patrol, U.S. Customs, CIA) and feel comfortable with them, seize the opportunity to ask them this question: "In what situation would you take up arms against an innocent and unarmed U.S. Citizen?" Answers you will not want to hear will include "When I am told to.", "When I feel it is my duty.", and "(blah, blah) Martial Law (blah, blah)" but, at the very least, it may give them pause to think about it (possibly for the first time since their initiation). You must understand that in most cases they have been chosen for their positions with specific regard for their disposition and have been specially conditioned for the coming attractions, whether or not they consciously realize it.

9.Be creative. Use your ingenuity and special/unique talents to do what you can.

10.When the scales begin to tip in our favor then I think you will know when to jump on for the final blow to the NWO and the Federal Reserve. But, there is no time like the present...

PLEASE WAKE UP, AMERICA!

THESE ARE THE ONLY TWO PRESIDENTS WHO EVER ATTEMPTED TO END THE FEDERAL RESERVE BANKING SYSTEM

WHAT ELSE DO THEY HAVE IN COMMON???

This information was via the Occupy New Zealand site on Facebook.
http://www.facebook.com/pages/Occupy-New-Zealand/229645187093918

The federal reserve system creates all of our money AS DEBT in the first place, it is where our money comes from, and the money is not given to our government, it is LOANED with INTEREST from the very beginning, meaning that ALL US DOLLARS THAT ARE EVER CREATED ARE LOANED AT INTEREST LIKE A CREDIT CARD, which creates the inevitable situation that THERE IS NEVER ENOUGH CURRENCY IN CIRCULATION TO PAY OFF THE DEBT, just like if you borrowed from a credit card, and then tried to pay off the credit card with more credit from the card, it makes no sense whatsoever. This means that our money system is A SCAM from the very beginning, the problem in our country is not simply that a few greedy people on Wall Street are stealing the money, it is that THE MONEY BY ITS VERY CREATION IS STEALING FROM THE PEOPLE IN THE FIRST PLACE, because when the banks come to collect on the phony debt they created, they get our ACTUAL WEALTH which is our houses, our cars, our land, etc etc etc, they create fake imaginary digits out of thin air with built-in interest, then collect our real wealth because there aren't enough units in circulation to pay off the interest.

As more and more people discover the emptiness of affluence and seek a meaningful life, growth and consumerism will fade in importance.

Happiness is less a matter of getting what we want, than of wanting what we have.
John Elliot 2011.

A few years ago we had Steve Jobs, Johhny Cash and Bob Hope.

Now we have no Jobs, no Cash and no Hope.

Climate Change and Global Warming

There is no debate in my book that the world faces unprecedented challenges as far as Climate Change and Global Warming goes, some or most of which can be blamed on human activity.

There has been some publicity mainly from oil companies trying to muddy the waters as far as climate change goes. But the evidence is overwhelming in the camp that we have to do something soon to save ourselves and planet Earth.

There was an interview on the radio this morning about the current situation (October 2011) being a perfect storm of events. On one hand we have floods, fires, earthquakes (Japan and Christchurch New Zealand), oil spills in the Gulf of Mexico and an oil spill currently in Tauranga New Zealand. Then we have the Global Financial Crisis and the lack of answers from the politicians and bankers. We also have the Arab Spring across the Middle East and protests around the world at grass root levels, protesting the greed of the rich and lack of employment especially for young people. There is melting of the ice caps at the polar regions and all in all it is not a great time for many people.

All these have come together as the world faces some stark choices about the future of Mankind and the Planet.

The interview also said that we mankind are very slow to adapt sometimes, but that the current situation as described may force a crisis that will spur Mankind into action. I sincerely hope it is sooner rather than later. The interview said that sometimes mankind only reacts when there is a major crisis. Perhaps that time is coming soon.

In America there are now 39 million people living in poverty, some have lost jobs, their superannuation nest eggs, their homes, their health care plans and their dignity. This situation can not continue, but then we have the Republicans and the Tea Party wanting no taxes, no government, no health care, no environmental rules and no banking rules. Also in America 1% of the population control 33% of the national wealth. Americans are 2% of the worlds population but they consume 25% of the worlds resources. But it is not just America it is all the countries of the world and now also China that faces major problems. We want a Rolls Royce lifestyle on a Mini-Minor income.

What sort of insane answer is that to what has happened in the last few years were liaise faire economics have been thoroughly discredited. Mr Warren Buffett says that taxes on the rich have to increase or there will be problems.

We need some sensible answers to the global problems we face, like a much more fairer distribution of wealth, employment and much tighter rules for banks and for protecting the environment. Short term ideas like bailing out banks and quantitative easing (burning money), as well as cutting wages, pensions and government services, and selling off state owned assets, are not an answer in the long term.

Also our environmental practices have to adapt to the new realities facing us. The idea of unending growth and consumption and the bad environmental practices like relying on more and more chemicals and more and more the use of fossil fuels can not continue. The status quo is not an option.

The news now is full of doom on the horizon if we do not tackle these issues with some long term sustainable solutions.

All these things that are happening around the globe are another reason why we should be prepared for tough times ahead.

"Infinite growth not feasible on a finite planet", Mike Ruppert.

OK, But What Do I Prepare For?

Before you can prepare, you must determine what you are preparing to survive and how each disaster threatens you, your safety and survival. That will give you the parameters necessary for the following steps.

This initial exercise isn't tough, it only takes a few minutes of thought. We suggest you jot notes or switch into your word processor while you work.

But first, it's important to realize that you cannot prepare for everything - only the army tries to do that, and we've yet to meet anyone with their resources. Captain Dave suggests you prepare only for those potential disasters that are likely to occur within the next five years. Sure, you may wait seven years for the next earthquake, but remember the survivalists creed: better safe than sorry.

What's going to happen in the next five years? If we knew, our web page would look different. You'll have to extrapolate, evaluate trends, read the newspaper, conduct your own research. At the very least, take a few minutes and consider your location. Pull out a map and look what's within a two-mile, five-mile 10-mile and 25-mile radius of your home and place of work. Put on your pessimist hat and consider what might go wrong that could directly impact you. Decide if that's something you want to prepare for (see questions one and two, below).

For example, if you live a "safe" distance outside of a flood plain, your house might still gets flooded in the 100-year flood, should you prepare for it? We would, but it's your call. It's your ass on the line, so you have to decide.

That nuclear plant 20 miles away has an excellent safety record. Should a nuclear disaster be on your list? Again, you make the call.

Are you worried about a meteorite crashing into your house? Well, it has happened, but it's probably not worth preparing for.

Finally, if you've been afraid of something since you were a child - whether it's a raging fire or nuclear war - prepare for it. At the very least, you'll sleep better at nights knowing you have done all you can.

Here are some questions to ask yourself:

What natural disasters or extreme conditions am I (we) l likely to face in the next five years?

Make a list and rank them in order of most to least likely to impact you. Your list might look like this:
Natural Disasters
Weather-related
Hurricanes Tornadoes Heavy thunder storms
Flash flooding Flooding Mud/rock slides
High winds Hail Severe winter weather
Avalanche Extreme high heat Drought
Wildfire
Non Weather-related
Earthquake Volcano eruption Tidal wave/Tsunami
Man-made Disasters

War (conventional, biological, chemical or nuclear)

Toxic material emission or spill (from a train, semi-truck or nearby plant)

Riot or other civil disorder Nuclear plant melt down or other nuclear disaster

Terrorism Fire Government action against you

Stock market crash Sever depression

Other

Plague or disease outbreak Comet strike or giant meteor

Personal Emergencies

Kidnapping Mugging, robbery or other criminal attack

Unemployment financial disaster

Death in family Home destroyed by fire

Random acts of violence

What are the ramifications of each item on my list.??

Now, take your list and create a second column. Put the ramifications of each disaster in the second

column. What do we mean by ramification? How the disaster or emergency situation could affect

you. Think this one through very carefully, as everyone's situation is different. For example, families with children have different concerns than those without or singles.

Potential Disaster Ramifications

Thunder storm with electrical outage for 2 (average) to 48 hours (severe)

Food spoilage possible

Lack of air conditioning/furnace

Damage to house or car from nearby trees

Possible local flooding (see below)

Local transportation impaired by fallen trees, wires

Lightning damage/fire potential

Severe winter weather, Electrical power outage for 4hrs (average) to 72 hours (severe)

Would affect furnace operation

Exposure problems

Frozen pipes

Disruption of travel, transportation

Self or family members possibly stranded away from home

Possible food shortages and empty shelves at local markets

Nearby flash flooding Local transportation disrupted

Danger while travelling in car or by foot

Possible loss of some utilities

Nearby train derailment Possible leak or spill of chemicals

Short-term exposure problem

Long-term cancer concerns

Evacuation may be necessary

Riot or other civil disorder Disruption of commute (ala Los Angeles)

Stranded in car or office while family is at home and/or school

Danger of riot spreading to my neighborhood

Danger of local kids/low lives taking advantage of situation
Attack or threat to personal safety
Looting and rampaging by otherwise lawful citizens
Fire with potentially no response by authorities
Police are overwhelmed, cannot protect law-abiding citizens
Nuclear plant problems
Reactor vessel damage could result in release of radioactive chemicals to atmosphere
Evacuation necessary
Terrorism Threat to safety at work and during business travel
Disruption of commerce, travel
Less personal freedom, privacy as a result of government reaction to terrorism
Once you've created a chart like the one above, you know what situations you are most likely to face and can prepare your survival plan.

Copyright 2005, Capt. Dave

Disaster Plan

Plan to look after yourself and your loved ones for at least 3 day or more

People do not plan to fail, they just fail to plan.

Many disasters will affect essential services and possibly disrupt your ability to travel or communicate with each other. You may be confined to your home, or forced to evacuate your neighbourhood. In the immediate aftermath of a disaster, emergency services will not be able to get help to everyone as quickly as needed.

This is when you are likely to be most vulnerable. So it is important to plan to look after yourself and your loved ones for at least three days or more in the event of a disaster.

Get your family or household together and agree on a plan. A functional emergency plan helps alleviate fears about potential disasters, and can help you respond safely and quickly when a disaster happens. You can get a copy of a household emergency plan and check list from your local council, or download your printable Household Emergency Plan template

A household emergency plan will help you work out:
What you will each do in the event of disasters such as an earthquake, tsunami, volcanic eruption, flood or storm.
How and where you will meet up during and after a disaster

Where to store emergency survival items and who will be responsible for maintaining supplies.

What you will each need to have in your getaway kits and where to keep them.

What you need to do for members of the household, family or community with a disability or special requirement.

What you will need to do for your pets, domestic animals or livestock.

How and when to turn off the water, electricity and gas at the main switches in your home or business.

Turn off gas only if you suspect a leak, or if you are instructed to do so by authorities. If you turn the gas off you will need a professional to turn it back on and it may take them weeks to respond after an event.

What local radio stations to tune in to for civil defence information during an event.

How to contact your local council's civil defence emergency management office for assistance during an emergency.

If life or property is threatened, always dial 111.

Ask the emergency management staff at your local council about your community's civil defence warning system, and the location of civil defence or public shelters. Check your council website for information on local civil defence arrangements.

It is also useful to learn first aid and how to deal with small fires.

TALKING TO CHILDREN ABOUT DISASTERS
Parents and caregivers should consider talking to children about the disasters that could happen in your community and what to do to keep safe. This can help to reduce fear and anxiety and helps everyone know how to respond.

INSURANCE
Make sure your insurance cover is adequate and up to date and that important documents can easily be gathered if you have to evacuate.

In most emergencies you should be able to stay in your home. Plan to be able to look after yourself and your household for at least three days or more. Assemble and maintain your emergency survival items for your home as well as a portable getaway kit in case you have to leave in a hurry. You should also have essential emergency items in your workplace and in your car.

EMERGENCY SURVIVAL ITEMS
Torch with spare batteries or a self-charging torch
Radio with spare batteries
Wind and waterproof clothing, sun hats, and strong outdoor shoes.
First aid kit and essential medicines
Blankets or sleeping bags
Pet supplies
Toilet paper and large rubbish bags for your emergency toilet
Face and dust masks

Check all batteries every three months. Battery powered lighting is the safest and easiest. Do not use candles as they can tip over in earthquake aftershocks or in a gust of wind. Do not use kerosene lamps, which require a great deal of ventilation and are not designed for indoor use.

Food and water for at least three days
Non-perishable food (canned or dried food)
Food, formula and drinks for babies and small children
Water for drinking. At least 3 litres per person, per day
Water for washing and cooking
A primus or gas barbeque to cook on
A can opener
Check and replace food and water every twelve months. Consider stocking a two-week supply of food and water for prolonged emergencies such as a pandemic.

GETAWAY KITS
In some emergencies you may need to evacuate in a hurry. Everyone should have a packed getaway kit in an easily accessible place at home and at work which includes:
Torch and radio with spare batteries
Any special needs such as hearing aids and spare batteries, glasses or mobility aids
Emergency water and easy-to-carry food rations such as energy bars and dried foods in case there are delays in reaching a welfare centre or a place where you might find support. If you have any special dietary requirements, ensure you have extra supplies
First aid kit and essential medicines
Essential items for infants or young children such as formula and food, nappies and a favourite toy
Change of clothes (wind/waterproof clothing and strong outdoor shoes)
Toiletries – towel, soap, toothbrush, sanitary items, toilet paper
Blankets or sleeping bags
Face and dust masks
Pet supplies
Include important documents in your getaway kit: identification (birth and marriage certificates, driver's licences and passports), financial documents (e.g. insurance policies and mortgage information), and precious family photos.

FIRST AID
If someone you care for is injured in a disaster, your knowledge of first aid will be invaluable. Many organisations provide first aid training courses. Consider taking a first aid course, followed by regular refresher sessions. You can buy ready-made first aid kits or make up your own.

For a list of providers for first aid courses and kits. Click here

First Aid Kit
You can buy First Aid Kits ready made. If you are making your own, these items are

recommended by St. John as the minimum required for families.
Triangular bandages (2)
Roller bandages- 50mm (1 roll) and 75 mm (1 roll)
Sterile gauze- 7.5 x 7.5 (2)
Adhesive wound dressing- 6 cm wide x 1 metre long (1 strip)
Plaster strip dressings (1 packet)
Adhesive tape- 25mm hypoallergenic (1 roll)
Sterile non-adhesive pads- small (2) and large (3)
Sterile eye pad
Eye wash container
Eye wash solution- Saline Steritube 30ml (1)
Antiseptic solution- Chlorhexidine Steritube 30ml (4)
Safety pins (1 card)
Scissors (1 pair)
Splinter forceps (1 pair)
Disposable gloves (2 pairs)
Accident register and pencil
First Aid Manual
Card listing local emergency numbers

HOW TO GET READY
1.Learn about the disasters that can affect you
2.Create and practice a household emergency plan
3.Assemble and maintain emergency survival items
4.Have a getaway kit in case you have to leave in a hurry

GET READY NOW SO YOU CAN GET THROUGH
Disasters such as earthquakes, tsunamis, volcanic eruptions, floods and storms can strike at any time, sometimes without warning. All disasters have the potential to cause disruption, damage property and take lives.

Get ready now to protect yourself, your family, home, business and community.

How To Get Ready
Household Emergency Plan
Emergency Survival Items and Getaway Kits
Evacuation
People with disabilities or special requirements
Pets and livestock
Storing water
Emergency sanitation
Get your car ready
Get your business ready
Who to contact

Radio Stations to listen to

Earthquake

Tsunami
Volcano
Flood
Storms
Landslide

HOUSEHOLD EMERGENCY PLAN
Plan to look after yourself and your loved ones for at least 3 days or more
Many disasters will affect essential services and possibly disrupt your ability to travel or communicate with each other. You may be confined to your home, or forced to evacuate your neighbourhood. In the immediate aftermath of a disaster, emergency services will not be able to get help to everyone as quickly as needed.

This is when you are likely to be most vulnerable. So it is important to plan to look after yourself and your loved ones for at least three days or more in the event of a disaster.

Get your family or household together and agree on a plan. A functional emergency plan helps alleviate fears about potential disasters, and can help you respond safely and quickly when a disaster happens. Make a start on your plan today. Use the plan template on page 18. Or get a copy of a household emergency plan and checklist from your local council, or download a copy from www.getthru.govt.nz

A household emergency plan will help you work out:
What you will each do in the event of disasters such as an earthquake, tsunami, volcanic eruption, flood or storm.
How and where you will meet up during and after a disaster.
Where to store emergency survival items and who will be responsible for maintaining supplies.
What you will each need to have in your getaway kits and where to keep them.
What you need to do for members of the household, family or community with a disability or special requirement.
What you will need to do for your pets, domestic animals or livestock.
How and when to turn off the water, electricity and gas at the main switches in your home or business. Turn off gas only if you suspect a leak, or if you are instructed to do so by authorities. If you turn the gas off, you will need a professional to turn it back on and it may take them weeks to respond after an event.
What local radio stations to tune in to for civil defence information during an event.
How to contact your local council's civil defence emergency management office for assistance during an emergency. If life or property is threatened, always dial 111.
Ask the civil defence emergency management staff at your local council about your community's civil defence warning system, and the location of civil defence or public shelters.

It is also useful to learn first aid and how to deal with small fires.

Talking to children about disasters

Parents and caregivers should consider talking to children about the disasters that could happen in your community and what to do to keep safe. This can help to reduce fear and anxiety and helps everyone know how to respond.

Insurance

Make sure your insurance cover is adequate and up to date and that important documents can easily be gathered if you have to evacuate.

EMERGENCY SURVIVAL ITEMS AND GETAWAY KITS

In most emergencies you should be able to stay in your home. Plan to be able to look after yourself and your household for at least three days or more. Assemble and maintain your emergency survival items for your home as well as a portable getaway kit in case you have to leave in a hurry. You should also have essential emergency items in your workplace and in your car.

Emergency Survival items

Torch with spare batteries or a self charging torch

Radio with spare batteries

Wind and waterproof clothing, sun hats, and strong outdoor shoes.

First aid kit and essential medicines

Blankets or sleeping bags

Pet supplies

Toilet paper and large rubbish bags for your emergency toilet

Face and dust masks

Check all batteries every three months. Battery powered lighting is the safest and easiest. Do not use candles as they can tip over in earthquake aftershocks or in a gust of wind. Do not use kerosene lamps, which require a great deal of ventilation and are not designed for indoor use.

Food and water for at least three days

Non-perishable food (canned or dried food)

Food, formula and drinks for babies and small children

Water (at least 3 litres per person per day) for drinking

Water for washing and cooking

A primus or gas barbeque to cook on

A can opener

Check and replace food and water every twelve months. Consider stocking a two-week supply of food and water for prolonged emergencies such as a pandemic.

Getaway Kits

In some emergencies you may need to evacuate in a hurry. Everyone should have a packed getaway kit in an easily accessible place at home and at work which includes:

Torch and radio with spare batteries

Any special needs such as hearing aids and spare batteries, glasses or mobility aids

Emergency water and easy-to-carry food rations such as energy bars and dried foods in case there are delays in reaching a welfare centre or a place where you might find support. If you have any special dietary requirements, ensure you have extra supplies

First aid kit and essential medicines

Essential items for infants or young children such as formula and food, nappies and a favourite toy

Change of clothes (wind/waterproof clothing and strong outdoor shoes)

Toiletries – towel, soap, toothbrush, sanitary items, toilet paper

Blankets or sleeping bags

Face and dust masks

Pet supplies

Include important documents in your kit: identification (birth and marriage certificates, driver's licences and passports), financial documents (e.g. insurance policies and mortgage information), and precious family photos.

First Aid

If someone you care for is injured in a disaster, your knowledge of first aid will be invaluable. Many organisations provide first aid training courses. Consider taking a first aid course, followed by regular refresher sessions.

You can buy ready-made first aid kits or make up your own. A list of the minimum recommended items for first aid kits can be downloaded from www.getthru.govt.nz

EVACUATION

In some situations you may be forced to evacuate your home, office, school or neighbourhood at short notice.

Before an evacuation

Find out about your community's warning systems and evacuation routes from civil defence emergency management staff at your local council.

Consider your transportation options in case you have to evacuate. If you do not own or drive a car, ask emergency management staff about plans for people without private vehicles.

Know which local radio stations to listen to during an event for announcements from your local emergency management officials.

Discuss and practice your evacuation plans with everyone in the household.

Make in-case-of-evacuation arrangements with friends or relatives in your neighbourhood as well as outside the area you are in.

Know the evacuation routes you could take and plan several evacuation routes in case roads are damaged or blocked.

Know where the emergency or welfare shelter locations are in your community

If you have pets, domestic animals or livestock, include them in your emergency plans.

If there is a possibility of an evacuation, fill your car's fuel tank. Keep in mind that if there are power cuts in an event, fuel stations may not be able to operate pumps.

If you are in an area that is being evacuated

Listen to your local radio stations as emergency management officials will be broadcasting the most appropriate advice for your community and situation.

Evacuate quickly if told to do so by authorities. Take your getaway kit with you. If you are outside the evacuation zone when a warning is issued, do not go into an at-risk area to collect your belongings.

If there is time, secure your home as you normally would when leaving for an extended period. Turn off electricity and water at the mains if there is time. Do not turn off natural gas unless you smell a leak or hear a blowing or hissing sound, or are advised to do so by the authorities.

Take your pets with you when you leave if you can safely do so.

If you have livestock, evacuate your family and staff first. If there is time, move livestock and domestic animals to a safer area.

In some emergency situations such as a tsunami or wildfire it is better to leave by foot than to drive or wait for transportation.

Use travel routes specified by local authorities. Some areas may be impassable or dangerous so avoid shortcuts. Do not drive through moving water. If you come upon a barrier, follow posted detour signs.

PEOPLE WITH DISABILITIES OR SPECIAL REQUIREMENTS

If you, or a member of your household or community has a disability or any special requirement that may affect the ability to cope in a disaster, make arrangements now to get the support needed.

Build a Personal Support Network

Organise a personal support network of a minimum of three people to alert you to civil defence warnings, or to help if you need to be evacuated. This could be family members, carers, friends, neighbours or co-workers.

Ensure you have an emergency plan before a disaster happens and practice it with your support network. Plan for various disasters and situations you could encounter.

Discuss your needs with the support network and make sure everyone knows how to operate necessary equipment.

Inform your support team if you are travelling or away from home.

Consider also

Ensuring you have emergency survival items, including any specialised items you need, and a getaway kit in case of evacuation.

Keeping at least seven days' supply of your essential medications and make provisions for those that require refrigeration.

Wearing a medical alert tag or bracelet to identify your disability or health condition.

When travelling, let a hotel or motel manager know of your requirements in case of an emergency.

Knowing where to go for assistance if you are dependent on a dialysis machine or other life-sustaining equipment or treatment.

Hearing impairment

Radio and television stations will broadcast civil defence information and advice before and during a disaster. Ask your support network to alert you to warnings and keep you informed.

Contact the emergency management staff at your local council to find out what local warning systems are in place in your community.

Consider installing a system appropriate to your needs such as an alarm with flashing strobe lights to get your attention. Replace the batteries once a year. You may want to consider giving a key to a neighbour so they can alert you to a warning. Keep a writing pad and pencils and a torch in your getaway kit so you can communicate with others.

Sight impairment
People who are blind or partially sighted may have to depend on others if they have to evacuate or go to an unfamiliar Civil Defence Centre. If you have a guide dog, make sure you have a getaway kit for your dog with food, medications, vaccination records, identification and harnesses to take with you. Keep extra canes at home and in the workplace even if you use a guide dog. Be aware that animals may become confused or disoriented in an emergency. Trained service animals will be allowed to stay in emergency shelters with their owners. Check with your local council for more information.

Physical disability or mobility impairment
If you or someone you are caring for has a physical disability or difficulty with mobility, include mobility aids in the emergency getaway kit. This will help in the event of an evacuation.
In a major earthquake the ground-shaking will make it difficult or impossible for you to move any distance. If you cannot safely get under a table, move near an inside wall of the building away from windows and tall items that can fall on you, and cover your head and neck as best you can. Lock your wheels if you are in a wheelchair. In bed, pull the sheets and blankets over you and use your pillow to protect your head and neck.

Asthma and respiratory problems
People with asthma or a respiratory disorder will be more susceptible to dust, volcanic ash, or the stress of an emergency. Make sure you have dust masks at home and in your emergency getaway kit and sufficient medicines for at least seven days.

Special food requirements
If you, or someone you are caring for, have special dietary needs, make sure there is sufficient stock of these food items for at least seven days at home, and in the emergency getaway kit. If you have to be evacuated, emergency shelters are unlikely to have the special food items you may need.

PETS AND LIVESTOCK
If you have pets, domestic animals or livestock, include them in your emergency planning.

Attach a permanent disc to your pet's collar that clearly states your phone number, name and address. Microchip your pets.
Ensure you have a carry box, towel or blanket, emergency food, and a lead and muzzle as part of your pet's emergency getaway kit. Put your name, phone number and address on the box.
In the event of an evacuation take your pets with you if you can safely do so. Take their vaccination records and essential medications with you as this will help your pet be re-housed

if necessary.

Welfare or civil defence centres generally will not accept pets except for service animals such as guide dogs. Some communities have established sheltering options for pets.

Make in-case-of-evacuation arrangements with friends or relatives outside your neighbourhood or area.

Keep a list of "pet-friendly" hotels and motels and their contact details in case you have to evacuate your home or neighbourhood.

If you have domestic animals (such as horses, pigs or poultry) or livestock, know which paddocks are safe to move livestock away from floodwaters, landslides and power lines. In the event of an evacuation, ensure you have a plan in place so that they will be secure and have food, water and shelter. The responsibility for animal welfare remains with the owner.

Check with your council about local arrangements for assisting with domestic animal issues.

STORING WATER

Household water supplies, including drinking water, could be affected in a disaster so having a supply of stored water is absolutely essential. You need at least three litres of drinking water for each person each day. You will also need water for washing and cooking.

You can purchase bottled water or prepare your own containers of water. Purchase food-grade water storage containers from camping or hardware stores or recycle plastic soft drink bottles. Do not use milk containers as protein cannot be adequately removed with washing, and may harbour bacteria.

Instructions for safely storing water

Wash bottles thoroughly in hot water.

Fill each bottle with tap water until it overflows.

Add five drops of household bleach per litre of water (or half a teaspoon for 10 litres) and put in storage. Do not drink for at least 30 minutes after disinfecting.

Label each bottle with dates showing when the bottles were filled and when they need to be refilled.

Check the bottles every 12 months. If the water is not clear, throw it out and refill clean bottles with clean water and bleach.

Store bottles away from direct sunlight in a cool dark place. Keep them in two separate places and where there is not likely to be flooding.

You can also fill plastic ice cream containers with water, cover, label and keep in the freezer. These can help keep food cool if the power is off and can also be used for drinking.

Your hot water cylinder and toilet cistern are valuable sources of water. Check that your hot water cylinder and header tank are well secured. Do not put chemical cleaners in the cistern if you want to use the water. If you use collected rain water make sure that you disinfect it with household bleach. If you are uncertain about the quality of water, e.g. from a well that has been flooded, or if it might have been contaminated by smoke or volcanic ash, do not drink it.

EMERGENCY SANITATION

In some emergency situations the water supply may be cut off, or water and sewage lines may be damaged, and you may need to use improvised emergency toilets.

How to make an emergency toilet

Use watertight containers such as a rubbish bin or bucket, with a snug-fitting cover.

If the container is small, keep a large container with a snug-fitting cover available for waste disposal.

Line bins with plastic bags if possible.

Pour or sprinkle a small amount of regular household disinfectant such as chlorine bleach into the container each time the toilet is used to reduce odour and germs. Keep the toilet covered.

GET YOUR CAR READY

Plan ahead for what you will do if you are in your car when a disaster strikes. In some emergencies you may be stranded in your vehicle for some time. A flood, snow storm or major traffic accident could make it impossible to proceed.

Consider having essential emergency survival items in your car. If you are driving in extreme winter conditions, add windshield scrapers, brush, shovel, tire chains and warm clothing to your emergency kit.

Store a pair of walking shoes, waterproof jacket, essential medicines, snack food, water and a torch in your car.

When planning travel, keep up-to-date with weather and roading information

GET YOUR BUSINESS READY

Under the Health and Safety in Employment Act, businesses have an obligation to be prepared for an emergency. Put together a Workplace Emergency Plan for your business.

Get your staff ready. Encourage staff to keep essential items they may need at work, including sturdy walking shoes, waterproof jacket, torch, snack food and water.

Get involved in business continuity and emergency plans at industry level. Your plans should cover these areas:

How to protect your business assets: staff, equipment, facilities, IT systems, reputation, market share, liquidity, etc.

How to protect external service, particularly in support of civil defence emergency management critical activities, such as emergency services and medical facilities.

Forecasting and prioritising external demand for your services before an emergency occurs.

Cooperative planning with those you depend on so that responsibilities and roles are clearly understood.

There is more information on Workplace Emergency Planning at www.civildefence.govt.nz.

WHO TO CONTACT

The primary responsibility for civil defence emergency management (CDEM) at a local level rests with your local council. Local and regional councils work with emergency services

(Police, Fire, Ambulance) and other relevant agencies to plan for, and respond to disaster events.

CDEM Groups are the consortium of local councils and agencies in each region and they have a responsibility to plan for, and manage regional hazards and risks.

Contact the civil defence emergency management office at your nearest local council for information on local hazards and community response arrangements.

During a disaster event telephone lines need to be kept clear for emergency calls to get through so please avoid making calls unless absolutely urgent.
If life or property is threatened always dial 111 for Police, Fire or Ambulance.

RADIO STATIONS TO LISTEN TO
The following radio networks work collaboratively with civil defence emergency management authorities to broadcast important information and advice in an emergency.
National Radio
Newstalk ZB
Classic Hits
More FM
Radio Live
IWI Radio

Ensure you have a battery operated radio. In an emergency find, and tune in to, your local radio station as they will broadcast official civil defence information that is appropriate for your community and situation. Record the bandwidth for your local stations in your Emergency Plan.

EARTHQUAKE
New Zealand lies on the boundary of the Pacific and Australian tectonic plates. Most earthquakes occur at faults, which are breaks extending deep within the earth, caused by movements of these plates. There are thousands of earthquakes in New Zealand every year, but most of them are not felt because they are either small, or very deep within the earth. Each year there are about 150 – 200 quakes that are big enough to be felt. A large, damaging earthquake could occur at any time, and can be followed by aftershocks that continue for days or weeks.
Most earthquake-related injuries and deaths result from falling debris, flying glass and collapsing structures such as buildings and bridges. Earthquakes can also trigger landslides, avalanches, flash floods, fires and tsunami.

Before an earthquake
Develop a Household Emergency Plan. Assemble and maintain your emergency survival Items for your home and workplace, as well as a portable getaway kit.
Practice Drop, Cover and Hold.
Identify safe places within your home, school or workplace. A safe place is:

somewhere close to you, no more than a few steps or less than three metres away, to avoid injury from flying debris.

under a strong table (hold on to the table legs to keep it from moving away from you).

next to an interior wall, away from windows and tall furniture that can fall on you (protect your head and neck with your arms).

Keep in mind that in modern homes, doorways are no stronger than any other part of the structure and usually have doors that can swing and injure you.

Check your household insurance policy for cover and amount.

Seek qualified advice to make sure your house is secured to its foundations and ensure any renovations comply with the New Zealand Building Code.

Secure heavy items of furniture to the floor or wall. Visit www.eq-iq.org.nz to find out how to quake-safe your home.

During an earthquake

If you are inside a building, move no more than a few steps, drop, cover and hold. Stay indoors till the shaking stops and you are sure it is safe to exit. In most buildings in New Zealand you are safer if you stay where you are until the shaking stops.

If you are in an elevator, drop, cover and hold. When the shaking stops, try and get out at the nearest floor if you can safely do so.

If you are outside, move no more than a few steps away from buildings, trees, street lights and power lines, then drop, cover and hold.

If you are at the beach or near the coast, drop, cover and hold then move to higher ground immediately in case a tsunami follows the quake.

If you are driving, pull over to a clear location, stop and stay there with your seatbelt fastened until the shaking stops. Once the shaking stops, proceed with caution and avoid bridges or ramps that might have been damaged.

If you are in a mountainous area or near unstable slopes or cliffs, be alert for falling debris or landslides.

After an earthquake

Listen to your local radio stations as emergency management officials will be broadcasting the most appropriate advice for your community and situation.

Expect to feel aftershocks.

Check yourself for injuries and get first aid if necessary. Help others if you can.

Be aware that electricity supply could be cut, and fire alarms and sprinkler systems can go off in buildings during an earthquake even if there is no fire. Check for, and extinguish, small fires.

If you are in a damaged building, try to get outside and find a safe, open place. Use the stairs, not the elevators.

Watch out for fallen power lines or broken gas lines, and stay out of damaged areas.

Only use the phone for short essential calls to keep the lines clear for emergency calls.

If you smell gas or hear a blowing or hissing noise, open a window, get everyone out quickly and turn off the gas if you can. If you see sparks, broken wires or evidence of electrical system damage, turn off the electricity at the main fuse box if it is safe to do so.

Keep your animals under your direct control as they can become disorientated. Take measures to protect your animals from hazards, and to protect other people from your animals.

If your property is damaged, take notes and photographs for insurance purposes. If you rent your property, contact your landlord and your contents insurance company as soon as possible.

TSUNAMI

New Zealand's entire coast is at risk of tsunami. A tsunami can violently flood coastlines, causing devastating property damage, injuries and loss of life.

A tsunami is a natural phenomenon consisting of a series of waves generated when a large volume of water in the sea, or in a lake, is rapidly displaced. A tsunami can be caused by large submarine or coastal earthquakes; underwater landslides which may be triggered by an earthquake or volcanic activity; large coastal cliff or lakeside landslides; or volcanic eruptions beneath or near the sea.

There are three distinct types of tsunami.

Distant tsunami are generated from a long way away, such as from across the Pacific in Chile. In this case, we will have more than three hours warning time for New Zealand.

Regional tsunami are generated between one and three hours travel time away from their destination. An eruption from an underwater volcano in the Kermadec Trench, to the north of New Zealand, could generate a regional tsunami.

Local tsunami are generated very close to New Zealand. This type of tsunami is very dangerous because we may only have a few minutes warning.

Tsunami warnings

Warning messages and signals about a possible tsunami can come from several sources – natural, official or unofficial.

Natural warnings

For a local source tsunami which could arrive in minutes there won't be time for an official warning. It is important to recognise the natural warning signs and act quickly.

If you are at the coast and experience any of the following:

Feel a strong earthquake that makes it hard to stand up, or a weak rolling earthquake that lasts a minute or more

See a sudden rise or fall in sea level

Hear loud and unusual noises from the sea

Move immediately to the nearest high ground, or as far inland as you can.

Official warnings

Official warnings are only possible for distant and regional source tsunami. Official warnings are disseminated by the Ministry of Civil Defence & Emergency Management to the national media, local authorities and other key response agencies. Your local council may also issue warnings through local media, siren and other local arrangements.

Unofficial/informal warnings

You may receive warnings from friends, other members of the public, international media and from the internet. Verify the warning only if you can do so quickly. If official warnings are available, trust their message over informal warnings.

Before a Tsunami
If you live in a coastal area, ask your council about your tsunami risk and local warning arrangements.
If you have a disability or special requirements, arrange with your support network to alert you of any warnings and emergency broadcasts.
Develop a household emergency plan and have a getaway kit ready.
Know where the nearest high ground is and how you will reach it. Plan to get as high up or as far inland as you can. Plan your escape route for when you are at home, as well as for when you may be working or holidaying near the coast.

During a tsunami
Take your getaway kit with you if possible. Do not travel into the areas at risk to get your kit or belongings.
Take your pets with you if you can do so safely.
Move immediately to the nearest higher ground, or as far inland as you can. If evacuation maps are present, follow the routes shown.
Walk or bike if possible and drive only if essential. If driving, keep going once you are well outside the evacuation zone to allow room for others behind you.
If you cannot escape the tsunami, go to an upper storey of a sturdy building or climb onto a roof or up a tree, or grab a floating object and hang on until help arrives.
Boats are usually safer in water deeper than 20 metres than if they are on the shore. Move boats out to sea only if there is time and it is safe to do so.
Never go to the shore to watch for a tsunami. Stay away from at-risk areas until the official all-clear is given.
Listen to your local radio stations as emergency management officials will be broadcasting the most appropriate advice for your community and situation.

After a tsunami
Continue to listen to the radio for civil defence advice and do not return to the evacuation zones until authorities have given the all-clear.
Be aware that there may be more than one wave and it may not be safe for up to 24 hours, or longer. The waves that follow the first one may also be bigger.
Check yourself for injuries and get first aid if needed. Help others if you can.
Do not go sightseeing
When re-entering homes or buildings, use extreme caution as flood waters may have damaged buildings. Look for, and report, broken utility lines to appropriate authorities.
If your property is damaged, take notes and photographs for insurance purposes. If you rent your property, contact your landlord and your contents insurance company as soon as possible.

VOLCANO
New Zealand is situated on the 'Ring of Fire', a geographic belt encircling the Pacific Ocean

and containing about 90% of the earth's volcanoes. Volcanoes usually have short active periods, separated by longer dormant periods. The three main types of volcanoes found in New Zealand are cone volcanoes such as Mounts Ruapehu and Taranaki; volcanic fields such as the ones found in the Auckland area; and calderas such as Lake Taupo.

Volcanoes produce a wide variety of hazards that can kill people and destroy property nearby as well as hundreds of kilometres away. Hazards include widespread ashfall, very fast moving mixtures of hot gases and volcanic rock, and massive lahars.

GNS Science is responsible for monitoring volcanic activity and setting alert levels. If a life-threatening eruption is likely to occur, a civil defence emergency will be declared and the areas at risk will be evacuated.

Before a volcanic eruption
Find out about the volcanic risk in your community. Ask your local council about emergency plans and how they will warn you of a volcanic eruption.
Practice your evacuation plan with members of the household.
Develop a household emergency plan. Assemble and maintain your emergency survival Items for your home as well as a portable getaway kit.
Include your pets and livestock in your emergency plan

When a volcanic eruption threatens
Listen to your local radio stations as emergency management officials will be broadcasting the most appropriate advice for your community and situation.
Put your emergency plan into action.
If you have a disability or need assistance, make contact with your support network and keep informed of civil defence advice.
Put all machinery inside a garage or shed, or cover with large tarpaulins to protect them from volcanic ash.
Bring animals and livestock into closed shelters to protect them from volcanic ash.
Protect sensitive electronics and do not uncover until the environment is totally ash-free.
Water supplies can be affected so it is a good idea to store drinking water in containers and fill bathtubs and sinks with water.
Check on friends and neighbours who may require special assistance.

During a volcanic eruption
Listen to the radio for civil defence advice and follow instructions.
If outside at the time of eruption, seek shelter in a car or building. If caught in volcanic ashfalls, wear a dust mask or use a handkerchief or cloth over your nose and mouth.
Stay indoors as volcanic ash is a health hazard, especially if you have respiratory difficulties such as asthma or bronchitis.
When indoors, close all windows and doors to limit the entry of volcanic ash. Place damp towels at thresholds.
Do not tie up phone lines with non-emergency calls.
If you have to go outside use protective gear such as masks and goggles and keep as much of your skin covered as possible. Wear eyeglasses, not contact lenses as these can cause corneal

abrasions.

Disconnect drainpipes/downspouts from gutters to stop drains clogging. If you use a rainwater collection system for your water supply, disconnect the tank.

Stay out of designated restricted zones.

After a volcanic eruption

Listen to your local radio stations for civil defence advice and follow instructions.

Stay indoors and away from volcanic ashfall areas as much as possible.

When it is safe to go outside, keep your gutters and roof clear of ash as heavy ash deposits can collapse your roof.

If there is a lot of ash in the water supply, do not use your dishwasher or washing machine.

Avoid driving in heavy ashfall as it stirs up ash that can clog engines and cause serious abrasion damage to your vehicle.

Keep animals indoors where possible, wash away ash on their paws or skin to keep them from ingesting the ash, and provide clean drinking water.

Use a mask or a damp cloth and eye protection when cleaning up. Moisten the ash with a sprinkler before cleaning.

Look for and report broken utility lines to appropriate authorities

If your property is damaged, take notes and photographs for insurance purposes. If you rent your property, contact your landlord and your contents insurance company as soon as possible.

FLOOD

Floods are New Zealand's number one hazard in terms of frequency, losses and declared civil defence emergencies. Floods can cause injury and loss of life, damage to property and infrastructure, loss of stock, and contamination of water and land.

Floods are usually caused by continuous heavy rain or thunderstorms but can also result from tsunami and coastal storm inundation. A flood becomes dangerous if:

the water is very deep or travelling very fast

the floods have risen very quickly

the flood water contains debris, such as trees and sheets of corrugated iron

Getting ready before a flood strikes will help reduce damage to your home and business and help you survive.

Before a Flood

Find out from your local council if your home or business is at risk from flooding. Ask about evacuation plans and local public alerting systems; how you can reduce the risk of future flooding to your home or business; and what to do with your pets and livestock if you have to evacuate.

Know where the closest high ground is and how to get there.

Develop a household emergency plan. Assemble and maintain your emergency survival Items for your home as well as a portable getaway kit.

Check your insurance policy to ensure you have sufficient cover.

During a flood or if a flood is imminent

Listen to your local radio stations as emergency management officials will be broadcasting the most appropriate advice for your community and situation.

If you have a disability or need support, make contact with your support network.

Put your household emergency plan into action and check your getaway kit. Be prepared to evacuate quickly if it becomes necessary.

Where possible, move pets inside or to a safe place, and move stock to higher ground.

Consider using sandbags to keep water away from your home.

Lift valuable household items and chemicals as high above the floor as possible.

Fill bathtubs, sinks and storage containers with clean water in case water becomes contaminated.

Turn off utilities if told to do so by authorities as it can help prevent damage to your home or community. Unplug small appliances to avoid damage from power surges.

Do not attempt to drive or walk through flood waters unless it is absolutely essential

After a flood

It may not be safe to return home even when the flood waters have receded. Continue to listen to your local radio station for civil defence instructions.

Help others if you can, especially people who may require special assistance.

Throw away food including canned goods and water that has been contaminated by flood water.

Avoid drinking or preparing food with tap water until you are certain it is not contaminated. If in doubt, check with your local council or public health authority.

Look for and report broken utility lines to appropriate authorities

If your property is damaged, take notes and photographs for insurance purposes. If you rent your property, contact your landlord and your contents insurance company as soon as possible.

STORMS

Major storms affect wide areas and can be accompanied by strong winds, heavy rain or snowfall, thunder, lightning, tornadoes and rough seas. They can cause damage to property and infrastructure, affect crops and livestock, disrupt essential services, and cause coastal inundation.

Severe Weather Watches and Warnings are issued by the MetService and available through the broadcast media, by email alerts, and at www.metservice.com

Before a storm

Develop a household emergency plan. Assemble and maintain your emergency survival Items for your home as well as a portable getaway kit if you have to evacuate.

Prepare your property for high winds. Secure large heavy objects or remove any item which can become a deadly or damaging missile. Get your roof checked regularly to make sure it is secure. List items that may need to be secured or moved indoors when strong winds are forecast.

Keep materials at hand for repairing windows, such as tarpaulins, boards and duct tape.

If you are renovating or building, make sure all work complies with the New Zealand building code which has specific standards to minimise storm damage.

If farming, know which paddocks are safe to move livestock away from flood waters, landslides and power lines.

When a warning is issued and during a storm

Stay informed on weather updates. Listen to your local radio stations as civil defence authorities will be broadcasting the most appropriate advice for your community and situation.

Put your household emergency plan into action and check your getaway kit in case you have to leave in a hurry.

Secure, or move indoors, all items that could get blown about and cause harm in strong winds.

Close windows, external and internal doors. Pull curtains and drapes over unprotected glass areas to prevent injury from shattered or flying glass.

If the wind becomes destructive, stay away from doors and windows and shelter further inside the house.

Water supplies can be affected so it is a good idea to store drinking water in containers and fill bathtubs and sinks with water.

Don't walk around outside and avoid driving unless absolutely necessary.

Power cuts are possible in severe weather. Unplug small appliances which may be affected by electrical power surges. If power is lost unplug major appliances to reduce the power surge and possible damage when power is restored.

Bring pets inside. Move stock to shelter. If you have to evacuate, take your pets with you.

Snowstorms

In a snowstorm, the primary concerns are the potential loss of heat, power and telephone service, and a shortage of supplies if storm conditions continue for more than a day. It is important for people living in areas at risk from snowstorms to consider the need for alternative forms of heating and power generation.

Avoid leaving home unless absolutely necessary when a snow warning is issued.

If you have to travel make sure you are well prepared with snow chains, sleeping bags, warm clothing and essential emergency items.

At home, check fuel supplies for woodburners, gas heaters, barbeques and generators.

Bring pets inside. Move domestic animals and stock to shelter.

If you are caught in your car or truck in a snowstorm stay in your vehicle. Run the engine every ten minutes to keep warm. Drink fluids to avoid dehydration. Open the window a little to avoid carbon monoxide poisoning. Make yourself visible to rescuers by tying a bright-coloured cloth to your radio aerial or door, and keeping the inside light on.

Tornadoes

Tornadoes sometimes occur during thunderstorms in some parts of New Zealand. A tornado is a narrow, violently rotating column of air extending downwards to the ground from the base of a thunderstorm. Warning signs include a long, continuous roar or rumble or a fast approaching cloud of debris which can sometimes be funnel shaped.

Alert others if you can.

Take shelter immediately. A basement offers the greatest safety. If underground shelter is not available, move to an interior room without windows on the lowest floor. Get under sturdy furniture and cover yourself with a mattress or blanket.

If caught outside, get away from trees if you can. Lie down flat in a nearby gully, ditch or low spot and protect your head.

If in a car, get out immediately and look for a safe place to shelter. Do not try to outrun a tornado or get under the vehicle for shelter.

After a storm

Listen to your local radio stations as emergency management officials will be broadcasting the most appropriate advice for your community and situation.

Check for injuries and help others if you can, especially people who require special assistance.

Look for and report broken utility lines to appropriate authorities.

Contact your local council if your house or building has been severely damaged.

If your property or contents are damaged take notes and photographs and contact your insurance company. Inform your landlord if there is damage to the rental property.

Ask your council for advice on how to clean up debris safely.

LANDSLIDE

Landslides are a serious geological hazard throughout much of New Zealand. A landslide is the movement of rock, soil and vegetation down a slope. Landslides can range in size from a single boulder in a rock fall to a very large avalanche of debris with huge quantities of rock and soil that can be spread across many kilometres.

Heavy rainfall or earthquakes can cause a landslide. Human activity, such as removal of trees and vegetation, steep roadside cuttings or leaking water pipes can also cause landslides. Most landslides occur without public warning and it's important to recognise the warning signs and act quickly.

Before a landslide

Getting ready before a landslide will help reduce damage to your home and business and help you survive.

Find out from your council if there have been landslides in your area before and where they might occur again.

Check for signs that the ground may be moving. These signs include:

Small slips, rock falls and subsidence at the bottom of slopes.

Sticking doors and window frames.

Gaps where frames are not fitting properly.

Outside fixtures such as steps, decks, and verandahs moving or tilting away from the rest of the house.

New cracks or bulges on the ground, road, footpath, retaining walls and other hard surfaces.

Tilting trees, retaining walls or fences.

Be alert when driving especially where there are embankments along roadsides. Watch the road for collapsed pavements, mud and fallen rocks.

If you think a landslide is about to happen
Act quickly. Getting out of the path of a landslide is your best protection.
Evacuate and take your Getaway Kit with you. Take your pets with you and move livestock to safe paddocks if you can safely do so.
Warn neighbours who might be affected and help those who may need assistance to evacuate.
Contact emergency services and your local council to inform them of the hazard.

After a landslide
Keep in mind that further landslides may occur. Stay away from affected sites until it has been properly inspected and authorities give the all-clear.
Look for and report broken utility lines to appropriate authorities
If your property or contents are damaged take notes and photographs when it is safe to do so.
Contact your insurance company and inform your landlord if there is damage to the rental property.

OTHER
What to do in a pandemic
For up to date information, see www.moh.govt.nz
What to in a fire
For fire readiness and response, see www.fire.org.nz
Bomb Threat / Terrorism
For information on criminal acts and terrorism, see www.police.govt.nz

Household Emergency Plan

Complete This Plan with ALL Members of Your Household

Your Household

Address	
Name	Phone numbers
Name	Phone numbers
Name	Phone numbers
Name	Phone numbers
Name	Phone numbers

1. If we can't get home or contact each other we will meet or leave a message at:

Name	Contact details
Name (back up)	Contact details
Name (out of town)	Contact details

2. The person responsible for collecting the children from school is:

Name	Contact details

3. Emergency Survival Items and Getaway Kit

Person responsible for checking water and food	
Items will be checked and replenished on: (check and replenish at least once a year)	Date:
The Getaway Kits are stored in the	

4. Radio station we will tune in to for local information during a CD emergency

Station	AM/FM frequency

5. Friends/neighbours who may need our help or who can help us

Name	Contact details
Name	Contact details

5. Friends/neighbours who may need our help or who can help us	
Name	Contact details

6. Important information about your house/dwelling

On a separate sheet of paper draw a plan of the house showing places to shelter in an earthquake or storm, exits and safe assembly areas and where to turn off water, electricity and gas.

IMPORTANT NUMBERS For police, fire or ambulance call 111

Police station	Medical Centre	Insurance
Vet/kennel/cattery	Electricity	Water
Gas	Electrician	Plumber
Builder	Council Emergency Helpline	
Other	Other	

EMERGENCY SURVIVAL ITEMS
Torch with spare batteries or a self-charging torch
Radio with spare batteries
Wind and waterproof clothing, sun hats, and strong outdoor shoes
First aid kit and essential medicines
Blankets or sleeping bags
Pet supplies
Emergency toilet - toilet paper and large rubbish bags
Face and dust masks
Check all batteries every 3 months.
Food and water for 3 days or more
Non-perishable food (canned or dried food)
Food, formula and drinks for babies and small children
Water (at least 3 litres per person, per day) for drinking
Water for washing and cooking
A primus or gas barbeque to cook on
A can opener
Consider stocking a two-week supply of food and water for prolonged emergencies such as a pandemic. Check and replace food and water every twelve months.

How to store water
Wash bottles thoroughly in hot water. Fill each bottle with tap water until it overflows. Add five drops of household bleach per litre of water (or half a teaspoon for 10 litres)
Store in a cool dark place and replace the water every 12 months

GETAWAY KITS
Everyone in the house should have a packed getaway kit in an easily accessible place which includes:
Torch and radio with spare batteries
Hearing aids and spare batteries, glasses or mobility aids
Emergency water and easy-to-carry food rations
Extra supplies of special dietary items
First aid kit and essential medicines
For infants or young children – formula and food, nappies
Change of clothes (wind/waterproof clothing and strong outdoor shoes)
Toiletries – towel, soap, toothbrush, sanitary items, toilet paper
Blankets or sleeping bags
Face and dust masks
Pet supplies
Important documents:
Identification (birth and marriage certificates/driver's licences and passports
Financial (insurance policies and mortgage)
precious family photos

If we have to evacuate we will:
Take our Getaway Kit
Turn off electricity and water
Turn off gas only if we suspect a leak or if asked to do so by the authorities
Take our pets with us

www.getthru.govt.nz

Thoughts On Disaster Survival, Post Katrina

The follow information was provided via several emails by a friend heavily involved in the New Orleans disaster of hurricane Katrina, during the course of the disaster itself. Many of the comments were LIVE to that moment in time....

I've had over 30 people staying with me since Sunday, evacuating from New Orleans and points south in anticipation of Hurricane Katrina. Only two families were my friends they told other friends of theirs that they knew a place where they could hole up, and so a whole bunch arrived here! I didn't mind, because there were six RV's and travel trailers, so we had enough accommodation. However, I've had the opportunity to see what worked - and what didn't - in their evacuation plans and bug-out kits, and I thought a few "lessons learned" might be appropriate to share here.

1.Have a bug-out kit ready at all times. Many of these folks packed at the last minute, grabbing whatever they thought they'd need. Needless to say, they forgot some important things (prescription medications, important documents, baby formula, diapers, etc.). Some of these things (e.g. prescriptions) obviously can't be stocked up against possible emergency need, but you can at least have a list in your bug-out kit of what to grab at the last minute before you leave!
2.Renew supplies in your bug-out kit on a regular basis. Batteries lose their charge. Foods have an expiration date. So do common medications. Clothes can get moldy or dirty unless properly stored. All of these problems were found with the folks who kept backup or bug-out supplies on hand, and caused difficulties for them.
3.Plan on needing a LOT more supplies than you think. I found myself with over 30 people on hand, many of whom were not well supplied and the stores were swamped with literally thousands of refugees, buying up everything in sight. I had enough supplies to keep myself going for 30 days. Guess what? Those supplies ended up keeping 30-odd people going for two days. I now know that I must plan on providing for not just myself, but others in need. I could have been selfish and said "No, these are mine" - but what good would that do in a real disaster? Someone would just try to take them, and then we'd have all the resulting unpleasantness. Far better to have extra supplies to share with others, whilst keeping your own core reserve intact (and, preferably, hidden from prying eyes!).

4.In a real emergency, forget about last-minute purchases. As I said earlier, the stores were swamped by thousands of refugees, as well as locals buying up last-minute supplies. If I hadn't had my emergency supplies already in store, I would never have been able to buy them at the last minute. If I'd had to hit the road, the situation would have been even worse, as I'd be part of a stream of thousands of refugees, most of whom would be buying (or stealing) what they needed before I got to the store.

5.Make sure your vehicle will carry your essential supplies. Some of the folks who arrived at my place had tried to load up their cars with a humongous amount of stuff, only to find that they didn't have space for themselves! Pets are a particular problem here, as they have to have air and light, and can't be crammed into odd corners. If you have to carry a lot of supplies and a number of people, invest in a small luggage trailer or something similar (or a small travel trailer with space for your goodies) - it'll pay dividends if the S really does HTF.

6.A big bug-out vehicle can be a handicap. Some of the folks arrived here with big pick-ups or SUV's, towing equally large travel trailers. Guess what? - on some evacuation routes, these huge combinations could not navigate corners very well, and/or were so difficult to turn that they ran into things (including other vehicles, which were NOT about to make way in the stress of an evacuation!). This led to hard feelings, harsh words, and at least one fist-fight. It's not a bad idea to have smaller, more maneuverable vehicles, and a smaller travel trailer, so that one can "squeeze through" in a tight traffic situation. Another point a big SUV or pickup burns a lot of fuel. This is bad news when there's no fuel available! (See point 10 below.)

7.Make sure you have a bug-out place handy. I was fortunate in having enough ground (about 1.8 acres) to provide parking for all these RV's and trailers, and to accommodate 11 small children in my living-room so that the adults could get some sleep on Sunday night, after many hours on the road in very heavy, slow-moving traffic. However, if I hadn't had space, I would have unhesitatingly told the extra families to find somewhere else - and there wasn't anywhere else here, that night. Even shops like Wal-Mart and K-Mart had trailers and RV's backed up in their parking lots (which annoyed the heck out of shoppers trying to make last-minute purchases). Even on my property, I had no trailer sewage connections, so I had to tell the occupants that if they used their onboard toilets and showers, they had to drive their RV's and trailers somewhere else to empty their waste tanks. If they hadn't left this morning, they would have joined long, long lines to do this at local trailer parks (some of which were so overloaded by visiting trailers and RV's that they refused to allow passers-by to use their dumping facilities).

8.Provide entertainment for younger children. Some of these families had young children (ranging from 3 months to 11 years). They had DVD's, video games, etc. - but no power available in their trailers to show them! They had no coloring books, toys, etc. to keep the kids occupied. This was a bad mistake.

9.Pack essentials first, then luxuries. Many of these folks had packed mattresses off beds, comforters, cushions, bathrobes, etc. As a result, their vehicles were grossly overloaded, but often lacked real essentials like candles, non-perishable foods, etc. One family (both parents are gourmet cooks) packed eighteen (yes, EIGHTEEN!!!) special pots and pans, which they were going to use on a two-burner camp stove... They were horrified by my suggestion that under the circumstances, a nested stainless-steel camping cookware set would be rather more practical. "What? No omelet pan?" Sheesh...

10.Don't plan on fuel being available en route. A number of my visitors had real problems finding gas to fill up on the road. With thousands of vehicles jammed nose-to-tail on four lanes of interstate, an awful lot of vehicles needed gas. By the time you got to a gas station, you were highly likely to find it sold out - or charging exorbitant prices, because the owners knew you didn't have any choice but to pay what they asked. Much better to leave with a full tank of gas, and enough in spare containers to fill up on the road, if you have to, in order to reach your destination.

11.Have enough money with you for at least two weeks. Many of those who arrived here had very little in cash, relying on check-books and credit cards to fund their purchases. Guess what? Their small banks down in South Louisiana were all off-line, and their balances, credit authorizations, etc. could not be checked - so many shops refused to accept their checks, and insisted on electronic verification before accepting their credit cards. Local banks also refused (initially) to cash checks for them, since they couldn't check the status of their accounts on-line. Eventually (and very grudgingly) local banks began allowing them to cash checks for not more than $50-$100, depending on the bank. Fortunately, I have a reasonable amount of cash available at all times, so I was able to help some of them. I'm now going to increase my cash on hand, I think... Another thing - don't bring only large bills. Many gas stations, convenience stores, etc. won't accept anything larger than a $20 bill. Some of my guests had plenty of $100 bills, but couldn't buy anything.

12.Don't be sure that a disaster will be short-term. My friends have left now, heading south to Baton Rouge. They want to be closer to home for whenever they're allowed to return. Unfortunately for them, the Governor has just announced the mandatory, complete evacuation of New Orleans, and there's no word on when they will be allowed back. It will certainly be several weeks, and it might be several months. During that period, what they have with them - essential documents, clothing, etc. - is all they have. They'll have to find new doctors to renew prescriptions; find a place to live (a FEMA trailer if they're lucky - thousands of families will be lining up for these trailers); some way to earn a living (their jobs are gone with New Orleans, and I don't see their employers paying them for not working when the employers aren't making money either); and so on.

13.Don't rely on government-run shelters if at all possible. Your weapons WILL be confiscated (yes, including pocket-knives, kitchen knives, and Leatherman-type tools); you will be crowded into close proximity with anyone and everyone (including some nice folks, but also including drug addicts, released convicts, gang types, and so on); you will be under the authority of the people running the shelter, who WILL call on law enforcement and military personnel to keep order (including stopping you leaving if you want to); and so on. Much, much better to have a place to go to, a plan to get there, and the supplies you need to do so on your own.

14.Warn your friends not to bring others with them!!! I had told two friends to bring themselves and their families to my home. They, unknown to me, told half-a-dozen other families to come too - "He's a good guy, I'm sure he won't mind!" Well, I did mind... but since the circumstances weren't personally dangerous, I allowed them all to hang around. However, if things had been worse, I would have been very nasty indeed to their friends (and even nastier to them, for inviting others without clearing it with me first!). If you are a place of refuge for your friends, make sure they know that this applies to them ONLY, not their other friends. Similarly, if you have someone willing to offer you refuge, don't presume on his/her hospitality by arriving with others unforewarned.

15. Have account numbers, contact addresses and telephone numbers for all important persons and institutions. My friends will now have to get new postal addresses, and will have to notify others of this their doctors, insurance companies (medical, personal, vehicle and property), bank(s), credit card issuer(s), utility supplier(s), telephone supplier(s), etc. Basically, anyone who sends you bills, or to whom you owe money, or who might owe you money. None of my friends brought all this information with them. Now, when they need to change postal addresses for correspondence, insurance claims, etc., how can they do this when they don't know their account numbers, what number to call, who and where to write, etc.?

16. Have portable weapons and ammo ready to hand. Only two of my friends were armed, and one of them had only a handgun. The other had a handgun for himself, another for his wife, a shotgun, and an evil black rifle - MUCH better! I was asked by some of the other families, who'd seen TV reports of looting back in New Orleans, to lend them firearms. I refused, as they'd never handled guns before, and thus would have been more of a danger to themselves and other innocent persons than to looters. If they'd stayed a couple of days, so that I could teach them the basics, that would have been different but they wouldn't, so I didn't. Another thing - you don't have to take your entire arsenal along. Firearms for personal defense come first, then firearms for life support through hunting (and don't forget the skinning knife!). A fishing outfit might not be a bad idea either (you can shoot bait!). Other than that, leave the rest of your guns in the safe (you do have a gun safe, securely bolted to the floor, don't you?), and the bulk ammo supplies too. Bring enough ammo to keep you secure, but no more. If you really need bulk supplies of guns and ammo, they should be waiting for you at your bug-out location, not occupying space (and taking up a heck of a lot of weight!) in your vehicle. (For those bugging out in my direction, ammo supply will NOT be a problem...)

17. Route selection is very, very important. My friends (and their friends) basically looked at the map, found the shortest route to me (I-10 to Baton Rouge and Lafayette, then up I-49 to Alexandria), and followed it slavishly. This was a VERY bad idea, as something over half-a-million other folks had the same route in mind... Some of them took over twelve hours for what is usually a four-hour journey. If they'd used their heads, they would have seen (and heard, from radio reports) that going North up I-55 to Mississippi would have been much faster. There was less traffic on this route, and they could have turned left and hit Natchez, MS, and then cut across LA on Route 84. This would have taken them no more than five or six hours, even with the heavier evacuation traffic. Lesson think outside the box, and don't assume that the shortest route on the map in terms of distance will also be the shortest route in terms of time.

18. The social implications of a disaster situation. Feedback from my contacts in the LSP and other agencies is very worrying. They keep harping on the fact that the "underclass" that's doing all the looting is almost exclusively Black and inner-city in composition. The remarks they're reporting include such statements as "I'm ENTITLED to this stuff!", "This is payback time for all Whitey's done to us", and "This is reparations for slavery!". Also, they're blaming the present confused disaster-relief situation on racism "Fo sho, if Whitey wuz sittin' here in tha Dome waitin' for help, no way would he be waitin' like we is!" No, I'm not making up these comments... they are as reported by my buddies. This worries me very much. If we have such a divide in consciousness among our city residents, then when we hit a SHTF situation, we're likely to be accused of racism, paternalism, oppression, and all sorts of other crimes just

because we want to preserve law and order. If we, as individuals and families, provide for our own needs in emergency, and won't share with others (whether they're of another race or not) because we don't have enough to go round, we're likely to be accused of racism rather than pragmatism, and taking things from us can (and probably will) be justified as "Whitey getting his just desserts". I'm absolutely not a racist, but the racial implications of the present situation are of great concern to me. The likes of Jesse Jackson, Al Sharpton, and the "reparations for slavery" brigade appear to have so polarized inner-city opinion that these folks are (IMHO) no longer capable of rational thought concerning such issues as looting, disaster relief, etc.

19.Implications for security. If one has successfully negotiated the danger zone, one will be in an environment filled, to a greater or lesser extent, with other evacuees. How many of them will have provided for their needs? How many of them will rely on obtaining from others the things they need? In the absence of immediate State or relief-agency assistance, how many of them will feel "entitled" to obtain these necessities any way they have to, up to and including looting, murder and mayhem? Large gathering-places for refugees suddenly look rather less desirable... and being on one's own, or in an isolated spot with one's family, also looks less secure. One has to sleep sometime, and while one sleeps, one is vulnerable. Even one's spouse and children might not be enough... there are always going to be vulnerabilities. One can hardly remain consciously in Condition Yellow while bathing children, or making love! A team approach might be a viable solution here .

20.Too many chiefs, not enough Indians" in New Orleans at the moment. The mayor has already blown his top about the levee breach: he claims that he had a plan in place to fix it by yesterday evening, but was overruled by Baton Rouge, who sent in others to do something different. This may or may not be true... My LSP buddies tell me that they're getting conflicting assignments and/or requests from different organizations and individuals. One will send out a group to check a particular area for survivors but when they get there, they find no-one, and later learn that another group has already checked and cleared the area. Unfortunately, in the absence of centralized command and control, the information is not being shared amongst all recovery teams. Also, there's alleged to be conflict between City officials and State functionaries, with both sides claiming to be "running things" and some individuals in the Red Cross, FEMA, and other groups appear to be refusing to take instructions from either side, instead (it's claimed) wanting to run their own shows. This is allegedly producing catastrophic confusion and duplication of effort, and may even be making the loss of life worse, in that some areas in need of rescuers aren't getting them. (I don't know if the same problems are occurring in Mississippi and/or Alabama, but I wouldn't be surprised if they were.) All of this is unofficial and off-the-record, but it doesn't surprise me to hear it. Moral of the story if you want to survive, don't rely on the government or any government agency (or private relief organization, for that matter) to save you. Your survival is in your own hands - don't drop it!

21.Long-term vision. This appears to be sadly lacking at present. Everyone is focused on the immediate, short-term objective of rescuing survivors. However, there are monumental problems looming, that need immediate attention, but don't seem to be getting it right now. For example: the Port of Louisiana is the fifth-largest in the world, and vital to the economy, but the Coast Guard is saying (on TV) that they won't be able to get it up and running for three to six months, because their primary focus is on search and rescue, and thereafter, disaster relief. Why isn't the Coast Guard pulled off that job now, and put to work right away on something this critical? There are enough Navy, Marine and Air Force units available now to take over rescue missions. Another example there are over a million refugees from the Greater New Orleans area floating around. They need accommodation and food, sure but most of them are now unemployed, and won't have any income at all for the next six to twelve months. There aren't nearly enough jobs available in this area to absorb this workforce. What is being done to find work for them, even in states remote from the problem areas? The Government for sure won't provide enough for them in emergency aid to be able to pay their bills. What about mortgages on properties that are now underwater? The occupants both can't and won't pay; the mortgage holders will demand payment; and we could end up with massive foreclosures on property that is worthless, leaving a lot of folks neck-deep in debt and without homes (even damaged ones). What is being done to plan for this, and alleviate the problem as much as possible? I would have thought that the State government would have had at least the skeleton of an emergency plan for these sorts of things, and that FEMA would have the same, but this doesn't seem to be the case. Why weren't these things considered in the leisurely days pre-disaster, instead of erupting as immediate and unanswered needs post-disaster?

22.Personal emergency planning. This leads me to consider my own emergency planning. I've planned to cover an evacuation need, and could probably survive with relative ease for between two weeks and one month but what if I had been caught up in this mess? What would I do about earning a living, paying mortgages, etc.? If I can't rely on the State, I for darn sure had better be able to rely on myself! I certainly need to re-examine my insurance policies, to ensure that if disaster strikes, my mortgage, major loans, etc. will be paid off (or that I will receive enough money to do this myself). I also need to provide for my physical security, and must ensure that I have supplies, skills and knowledge that will be "marketable" in exchange for hard currency in a post-disaster situation. The idea of a "team" of friends with (or to) whom to bug out, survive, etc. is looking better and better. Some of the team could take on the task of keeping a home maintained (even a camp-type facility), looking after kids, providing base security, etc. Others could be foraging for supplies, trading, etc. Still others could be earning a living for the whole team with their skills. In this way, we'd all contribute to our mutual survival and security in the medium to long term. Life might be a lot less comfortable than prior to the disaster, but hey - we'd still have a life! This bears thinking about, and I might just have to start building "team relationships" with nearby [people of like mind]!

23.The "bank problem." This bears consideration. I was at my bank this morning, depositing checks I'd been given by my visitors in exchange for cash. The teller warned me bluntly that it might be weeks before these checks could be credited to my account, as there was no way to clear them with their issuing banks, which were now under water and/or without communications facilities. He also told me that there had been an endless stream of folks trying to cash checks on South Louisiana banks, without success. He warned me that some of these local banks will almost certainly fail, as they don't have a single branch above water, and the customers and businesses they served are also gone - so checks drawn on them will eventually prove worthless. Even some major regional banks had run their Louisiana "hub" out of New Orleans, and now couldn't access their records. I think it might be a good idea to have a "bug-out bank account" with a national bank, so that funds should be available anywhere they have a branch, rather than keeping all one's money in a single bank (particularly a local one) or credit union. This is, of course, over and above one's "bug-out stash" of ready cash.

24.Helping one's friends is likely to prove expensive. I estimate that I'm out over $1,000 at the moment, partly from having all my supplies consumed, and partly from making cash available to friends who couldn't cash their checks. I may or may not get some of this back in due course. I don't mind it - if I were in a similar fix, I hope I could lean on my friends for help in the same way, after all! - but I hadn't made allowance for it. I shall have to do so in future, as well as planning to contribute to costs incurred by those who offer me hospitality under similar circumstances.

25.People who were prepared were frequently mobbed/threatened by those who weren't. This was reported in at least seven incidents, five in Mississippi, two in Louisiana (I suspect that the relative lack of Louisiana incidents was because most of those with any sense got out of Dodge before the storm hit). In each case, the person/family concerned had made preparations for disaster, with supplies, shelter, etc. in good order and ready to go.

Several had generators ready and waiting. However, their neighbors who had not prepared all came running after the disaster, wanting food, water and shelter from them. When the prepared families refused, on the grounds that they had very little, and that only enough for themselves, there were many incidents of aggression, attempted assault, and theft of their supplies. Some had to use weapons to deter attack, and in some cases, shots were fired. I understand that in two incidents, attackers/would-be thieves were shot. It's also reported that in all of these cases, the prepared families now face threats of retribution from their neighbors, who regarded their refusal to share as an act of selfishness and/or aggression, and are now threatening retaliation. It's reportedly so bad that most of the prepared families are considering moving to other neighborhoods so as to start afresh, with different neighbors.

Similar incidents are reported by families who got out in time, prepared to spend several days on their own. When they stopped to eat a picnic meal at a rest stop, or an isolated spot along the highway, they report being approached rather aggressively by others wanting food, or fuel, or other essentials. Sometimes they had to be rather aggressive in their turn to deter these insistent requests. Two families report attempts being made to steal their belongings (in one case, their vehicle) while over-nighting in camp stops on their way out of the area. They both instituted armed patrols, with one or more family members patrolling while the others slept, to prevent this. Seems to me to be a good argument to form a "bug-out team" with like-minded, security-conscious friends in your area, so that all concerned can provide mutual security and back-up.

My take I can understand these families being unwilling to share the little they had, particularly in light of not knowing when supplies would once again be available. However, this reinforces the point I made in my "lessons learned" post last week plan on needing much more in the way of supplies than you initially thought! If these families had had some extra food and water in stock, and hidden their main reserve where it would not be seen, they could have given out some help to their neighbors and preserved good relations. Also, a generator, under such circumstances, is a noisy (and bright, if powering your interior lights) invitation saying "This house has supplies - come and get them". I suspect that kerosene lanterns, candles and flashlights might be a more "community-safe" option if one is surrounded by survivors.

26.When help gets there, you may get it whether you like it or not. There are numerous reports of aggressive, overbearing behavior by those rescuers who first arrived at disaster scenes. It's perhaps best described as "I'm here to rescue you - I'm in charge - do as I say - if you don't I'll shoot you". It appears that mid-level State functionaries and Red Cross personnel (the latter without the "shoot you" aspect, of course) were complained about most often. In one incident, a family who had prepared and survived quite well were ordered, not invited, to get onto a truck, with only the clothes on their backs. When they objected, they were threatened. They had pets, and wanted to know what would happen to them and they report that a uniformed man (agency unknown) began pointing his rifle at the pets with the words "I'll fix that". The husband then trained his own shotgun on the man and explained to him, in words of approximately one syllable, what was going to happen to him if he fired a shot. The whole "rescuer" group then left, threatening dire consequences for the family (including threats to come back once they'd evacuated and torch their home). The family were able to make contact with a State Police patrol and report the incident, and are now determined that no matter how much pressure is applied, they will not evacuate. They've set up a "shuttle run" so that every few days, two of them go upstate to collect supplies for the rest of the family, who defend the homestead in the meantime. Another aspect of this is that self-sufficient, responsible families were often regarded almost with suspicion by rescuers. The latter seemed to believe that if you'd come through the disaster better than your neighbors, it could only have been because you stole what you needed, or somehow gained some sort of unfair advantage over the "average victims" in your area. I'm at a loss to explain this, but it's probably worth keeping in mind.

27. There seems to be a cumulative psychological effect upon survivors. This is clear even or perhaps particularly - in those who were prepared for a disaster. During and immediately after the disaster, these folks were at their best, dealing with damage, setting up alternative accommodation, light, food sources, etc. However, after a few days in the heat and debris (perhaps worst of all being the smell of dead bodies nearby), many found their ability to remain positive and "upbeat" being strained to the limit. There are numerous reports of individuals becoming depressed, morose and withdrawn. This seemed to happen to even the strongest personalities. The arrival of rescuers provided a temporary boost, but once evacuated, a sort of "after-action shell-shock" seems to be commonly experienced. I don't know enough about this to comment further, but I suspect that staying in place has a lot to do with it - there is no challenge to keep moving, find one's survival needs, and care for the group, and one is surrounded by vivid reminders of the devastation. By staying among the ruins of one's former life, one may be exposing oneself to a greater risk of psychological deterioration.

28. There is widespread frustration over the lack of communication and empathy by rescuers and local/State government. This is partly due to the absence of electricity, so that TV's were not available to follow events as they unfolded but it's also due to an almost deliberate policy of non-communication by rescuers. There are many accounts of evacuees wanting to know where the bus or plane was going that they were about to board, only to be told "We don't know", or "To a better place than this". Some have found themselves many States away from their homes.

Other families were arbitrarily separated upon rescue and/or evacuation, and are still scattered across two or three States.

Their efforts to locate each other are very difficult, and when they request to be reunited at a common location, all of those with whom I have contact report a blanket refusal by the Red Cross and State officials to even consider the matter at this time. They're being informed that it will be "looked into" at some future date, and that they may have to pay the costs involved if they want to join up again. This, to families who are now destitute! I'm very angry about this, but it's so widespread a problem that I don't know what can be done about it. I hope that in future, some means will be implemented to prevent it happening again. Lesson learned never, EVER allow yourselves to be separated as a family, even if it means waiting for later rescue and/or evacuation. Insist on this at all costs!

29. Expect rescuers (including law enforcement) to enforce a distinctly un-Constitutional authority in a disaster situation. This is very widely reported, and is very troubling. I hear repeated reports from numerous States that as evacuees arrive at refugee centers, they and their belongings are searched without Constitutional authority, and any personal belongings seen as potentially suspicious (including firearms, prescription medication, etc.) are confiscated without recourse to the owner. I can understand the point of view of the receiving authorities, but they are acting illegally, and I suspect there will be lawsuits coming from this practice. Another common practice reported on the ground in the disaster areas is for people to be ordered to evacuate, irrespective of their needs and wishes - even those folks who were well-prepared and have survived in good shape. If they demur, they are often threatened and bullied in an attempt to make them abandon their homes, pets, etc. Lesson learned in a disaster, don't expect legal and Constitutional norms to be followed. If you can make it on your own, do so, without relying on an unsympathetic and occasionally overbearing rescue system to control you and your destiny.

30. Don't believe that rescuers are all knights in shining armor who will respect your property. There have been numerous reports of rescuers casually appropriating small items that took their fancy in houses they were searching. Sometimes this was blatant, right in front of onlookers, and when protests were made, the response was either threatening, or a casual "Who's going to miss it now?". Some of our field agents report that this happened right in front of their eyes. Another aspect of this is damage caused to buildings by rescuers. I've had reports of them kicking in the front door to a house, or a window, instead of trying to obtain access with as little damage as possible; climbing on clean, highly-polished tables with hobnailed boots in order to get at an attic hatch to check for survivors; etc. When they left the house, often the door or window was left open, almost a standing invitation to looters, instead of being closed and/or secured. When the families concerned get home, they won't know who caused this damage, but they will certainly be angered by it. I think that if one evacuates one's home, it might be a good idea to leave a clearly-visible notice that all residents have evacuated, so as to let would-be rescuers know that this house is empty. On the other hand, this might make it easier for looters, so what you gain on the swings, you lose on the round-abouts...

31. If you choose to help, you may be sucked into a bureaucratic and legal nightmare. Example: a local church in the beginning stages of the crisis offered its hall to house evacuees. Local and State officials promptly filled it up with over 100 people. Their "social skills" proved extremely difficult to live with... toilets were blocked, restrooms left filthy, graffiti were scrawled and/or carved on the walls, arguments and disputes were frequent (often escalating to screaming matches, sometimes to physical violence), evacuees roamed the neighborhood (leading to all sorts of reports of petty theft, vandalism, etc.), church workers were subject to aggressive begging and demands, etc. Requests to the authorities to provide better security, administrative assistance, etc. apparently fell on deaf ears - the crisis was so widespread and overwhelming that a small facility such as this seems to have been very low on the priority checklist. After two days of this, with complaints from the neighbors becoming more and more insistent, the

church informed local officials that it wanted the evacuees removed at once, if not sooner. They were promptly subject to bureaucratic heavy-handedness (including threats to withhold previously-promised reimbursement for their expenses); threats of lawsuits for daring to insinuate that the evacuees were somehow "lower-class" in their conduct, and for alleged racism, slander, and general political incorrectness; and threats of negative publicity, in that officials threatened to put out a press release denouncing the church for its "elitist" and "un-co-operative" attitude in a time of crisis. The church initially caved in to this pressure, and allowed the evacuees to stay but within a couple more days, the pressure from neighbors and from its own members became impossible to bear, and they insisted on the evacuees being removed to a Red Cross shelter. I'm informed that repairs to their hall will cost over $10,000. This is only one example among many I could cite, but it makes the point clear - if you offer your facilities to authorities, you place yourself (to a certain extent) under their control, and you're potentially liable to a great deal of heavy-handed, insensitive bureaucratic bullying. Those of you in the same position as this church (i.e. with facilities you could make available) might wish to take note.

32. Law enforcement problems will often be "glossed over" and/or ignored by authorities. In many cities housing evacuees, there have been private reports of a significant increase in crime caused by their presence but you'll find that virtually all law enforcement authorities publicly deny this and/or gloss over it as a "temporary problem". This is all very well for publicity, but it ignores the increased risk to local residents. I've been tracking crime reports in about a dozen cities, through my contacts with local law enforcement and the Louisiana State Police. All the LEO's I speak with, without exception, tell me of greatly increased crime, including rape, assault, robbery, shoplifting, vandalism, gang activity, etc. However, you won't see these reports in the news media, and will often see senior LE figures actively denying it. The officers with whom I speak are angry and bitter about this, but they daren't "go public", as their jobs would be on the line if they did so. They tell me that often they're instructed not to report certain categories of "incident" at all, so as not to "skew" or "inflate" the "official" crime figures. I've also heard reports from Texas, Alabama and Tennessee of brand-new high-end motor vehicles (e.g. Cadillacs, Lincolns, BMW's, etc.) with New Orleans dealer tags being driven through various towns, on their way North and West. The drivers were described as "gang-bangers" (and sundry less complimentary terms). However, there have been no reports of stolen vehicles from New Orleans, because there are no workers to check out dealer lots, or report thefts, and no working computers to enter VIN's, etc. into the NICS database of stolen vehicles - so officers have had no choice but to let these vehicles proceed. Draw your own conclusions.

33. Your personal and/or corporate supplies and facilities may be commandeered without warning, receipt or compensation. I've had numerous reports from in and near the disaster zone of individuals (e.g. boat-owners, farmers with barns, tractors, etc.) and corporate groups (e.g. companies with heavy equipment, churches with halls, etc.) finding an official on their doorstep demanding the use of their facilities or equipment. If they demurred, they were told that this was an "emergency situation" and that their assistance was being required, not requested. Some of them have lost track of the heavy equipment "borrowed" in this way, and don't know where it is, whether or not it's still in good condition, and when (if ever) it will be returned - and in the meantime, they can't continue their normal operations without this equipment. Others have had

their land and facilities effectively confiscated for use by rescue and relief workers, storage of supplies, etc. In some cases, in the absence of their owners, the property of the individuals and groups concerned (e.g. farm gasoline and diesel supplies, the inventory of motor vehicle dealers, suppliers of foodstuffs, tarpaulins, etc.) have been commandeered and used by law enforcement and relief workers, without permission, receipts, reimbursement, etc. Protests have been met with denials, threats of arrest, insinuations of being "uncaring" and "un-co-operative", etc. Lesson learned if you've got what officials need in a time of crisis, forget about Constitutional protections of your property! Sure, you can sue after the fact, but if you need your goods and facilities for your own survival, you're basically SOL. Those of us who stockpile necessities for potential crises like this might want to consider concealing our stockpiles to prevent confiscation and if you need certain equipment for your own day-to-day use (e.g. tractors for farmers, generators, etc.), you might have a hard time retaining possession of these things. This problem applies to relief workers also I've had several reports of private relief workers (e.g. those sent in by churches, etc.) having their vehicles and supplies commandeered by "official" relief workers, without compensation or receipt, and being kicked out of the disaster area with warnings not to return. The fact that the "private" workers were accomplishing rather more than the "official" workers was apparently of no importance.

34.If you look like you know what you're doing, you may be a target of those less prepared. There have been many, many reports of individuals who were more or less prepared for a disaster being preyed upon by those who were not prepared. Incidents range from theft of supplies, through attempts to bug out with these persons (uninvited), to actual violence. It's genuinely frightening to hear about these incidents, particularly the attitude of those trying to prey on the prepared they seemed to feel that because you'd taken steps to protect yourself and your loved ones, you had somehow done so at their expense, and they were therefore "entitled" to take from you what they needed. There's no logical explanation for this attitude, unless it's bred by the utter dependence of many such people on the State for welfare, Social Security, Medicare/Medicaid, etc. Since they've always been dependent on others, and regarded this as an "entitlement", in a disaster situation, they seem to automatically assume that they're "entitled" to what you've got! In one case, the family's pet dog was held hostage, with a knife at its throat, until the family handed over money and supplies. In two cases, families were threatened with the rape of their women unless they co-operated with the aggressors. In four cases that I know of, children were held hostage to ensure co-operation. There have also been reports of crimes during the bug-out process. Families sleeping in their cars at highway rest areas were a favorite target, including siphoning of gas from their tanks, assaults, etc. The lessons to be learned from this are obvious. One family can't secure itself against these threats without great difficulty. It's best to be "teamed up" with neighbors to secure your neighborhood as a whole, rather than be the one house with facilities in an area filled with those less prepared. If you're in the latter situation, staying put may not be a safe option, and a bug-out plan may be vital. When bugging out, you're still not safe from harm, and must maintain constant vigilance.

35.Those who thought themselves safe from the disaster were often not safe from refugees. There have been many reports of smaller towns, farms, etc. on the fringe of the disaster area being overrun with those seeking assistance. In many cases, assistance was demanded rather than requested, and theft, looting and vandalism have been reported. So, even if you think you're safe from the disaster, you may not be safe from its aftermath.

36.Self-reliance seems to draw suspicion upon you from the authorities. I've mentioned this in a previous e-mail, but I've had many more reports of it from those who survived or bugged out, and it bears re-emphasizing. For reasons unknown and unfathomable, rescue authorities seem to regard with suspicion those who've made provision for their safety and have survived (or bugged out) in good shape. It seems to be a combination of "How could you cope when so many others haven't?", "You must have taken advantage of others to be so well off", and "We've come all this way to help, so how dare you not need our assistance?" I have no idea why this should be the case... but there have been enough reports of it that it seems to be a widespread problem. Any ideas from readers?

37.Relief workers from other regions and States often don't know local laws. This is a particular problem when it comes to firearms. I've had many reports of law enforcement officers sent to assist in Louisiana from States such as New Jersey, California, etc. trying to confiscate firearms on the streets, etc., when in fact the armed citizens were legally armed, under local law. One can't reason with these officers in the heat of the moment, of course, and as a result, a number of people lost their firearms, and have still not recovered them (and in the chaos of the immediate post disaster situation, they may never do so, because I'm not sure that normal procedures such as logging these guns into a property office, etc. were followed). I understand that in due course, steps were taken to include at least one local law enforcement officer in patrols, so that he could advise officers from other areas as to what was legal, and what wasn't. Also, in Louisiana, law enforcement is conducted differently than in some other States, and officers from other States who came to assist were sometimes found to be domineering and aggressive in enforcing a law enforcement "authority" that doesn't normally apply here. So, if you're in a disaster area and help arrives from elsewhere, you may find that the help doesn't know (or care) about local laws, norms, etc. Use caution!

38.Relief organizations have their own bureaucratic requirements that may conflict with your needs. A good example is the Red Cross. In many cases, across three States, I've had reports that locals who needed assistance were told that they had to register at a particular Red Cross shelter or facility. The help would not come to them they had to go to it. If they wished to stay on their own property, they were sometimes denied assistance, and told that if they wanted help, they had to move into the shelter to get it. Also, assistance was often provided only to those who came in person. If you left your family at home and went to get food aid, you might be denied aid for your whole family because there was no evidence that they existed - only the number that could be physically counted by relief workers (who would not come to you, but insisted you come to them) would be provided with food. Needless to say, this caused much anger and resentment.

I hope that these "lessons learned" are of use to you. I'm more and more convinced that in the event of a disaster, I must rely on myself, and a few friends, and never count on Government or relief organizations for the help I'll need. Also, I'm determined to bug out for a fairly long distance from a disaster in my home area, so as to be clear of the post-disaster complications that may arise. Once again (as it has countless times throughout history), we see that to rely on others (let alone Government) for your own safety and security is to invite complications at best, disaster at worst.

From the LDS Preparedness Manual

PREPAREDNESS TEST

1.Has your family rehearsed fire escape routes from your home?
YES - NO
2. Does your family know what to do before, during, and after an earthquake or
YES - NO
other emergency situation?
3.Do you have heavy objects hanging over beds that can fall during an earthquake?
YES - NO
4.Do you have access to an operational flashlight in every occupied bedroom?
(use of candles is not recommended unless you are sure there is no leaking gas)
YES - NO
5.Do you keep shoes near your bed to protect your feet against broken glass?
YES - NO
6.If a water line was ruptured during an earthquake, do you know how to shut off the main
water line to your house?
YES - NO
7.Can this water valve be turned off by hand without the use of a tool?
Do you have a tool if one is needed?
YES - NO
8.Do you know where the main gas shut-off valve to your house is located?
YES - NO
9.If you smell gas, do you know how and would you be able to shut off this valve?
YES - NO
10.Gas valves usually cannot be turned off by hand. Is there a tool near your valve?
YES - NO
11.Would you be able to safely restart your furnace when gas is safely available?
YES - NO
12.Do you have working smoke alarms in the proper places to warn you of fire?
YES - NO
13.In case of a minor fire, do you have a fire extinguisher that you know how to use?
YES - NO
14.Do you have duplicate keys and copies of important insurance and other papers stored
outside your home?
YES - No
15.Do you have a functional emergency radio to receive emergency information?
YES - NO
16.If your family had to evacuate your home, have you identified a meeting place?
YES - NO
IF AN EMERGENCY LASTED FOR THREE DAYS (72 HOURS) BEFORE HELP WAS

AVAILABLE TO YOU AND YOUR FAMILY

17. Would you have sufficient food?
YES - NO

18. Would you have the means to cook food without gas and electricity?
YES - NO

19. Would you have sufficient water for drinking, cooking, and sanitary needs?
YES - NO

20. Do you have access to a 72 hour evacuation kit?
YES - NO

21. Would you be able to carry or transport these kits?
YES - NO

22. Have you established an out-of-state contact?
YES - NO

23. Do you have a first aid kit in your home and in each car?
YES - NO

24. Do you have work gloves and some tools for minor rescue and clean up?
YES - NO

25. Do you have emergency cash on hand? (During emergencies banks and ATMs are closed)
YES - NO

26. Without electricity and gas do you have a way to heat at least part of your house?
YES - NO

27. If you need medications, do you have a month's supply on hand?
YES - NO

28. Do you have a plan for toilet facilities if there is an extended water shortage?
YES - NO

29. Do you have a supply of food, clothing, and fuel where appropriate:
For 6 months? For a year?
YES - NO

These are all questions that need answers if you are to be safe in an emergency.

If you answered 'No' to any of them, its now time to work on getting those items done.

Glen Afton, Waikato, New Zealand Aotearoa

I have brought a section in Glen Afton in the Waikato New Zealand for $NZ20,000. The section is 863m2 or about 1/5 of an acre.

SA66A/350
Waikato District

Aerial Photo plus Property Boundaries $16.50   Not Available

Glen Afton NZ is an ex coal mining town that is now just a rural village with some houses and very few services or amenities.

There is one large and one small open cast coal mines still operating in the area.

The nearest town is Huntly NZ. Huntly is about 14km and 15 minutes drive from Glen Afton. The region is the Waikato and the nearest city is Hamilton NZ.

Glen Afton has a Dairy (Store) and a Club Rooms (The Blue Room). There is a Primary School at Pukemiro (The next Village).

There is the Bush Railway and the Country Music Club meets at the Club Rooms.
http://www.bushtramwayclub.com

There was a mining disaster at Glen Afton in 1939. Glen Afton mine, Huntly, 24 September 1939: 11 men were asphyxiated by carbon monoxide. Alan Sherwood and Jock Phillips. 'Coal and coal mining - Mining accidents', Te Ara - the Encyclopedia of New Zealand, updated 26-

Nov-10 URL: http://www.TeAra.govt.nz/en/coal-and-coal-mining/7

The roads in the area are good and mostly sealed. There is no public transport.

Land and House prices are quite cheap because of Glen Aftons location and the lack of amenities and services. Also Rates (Land Taxes) are quite mild as again there is little in the way of facilities.

The locals seem to be rugged individuals probably a lot of them are unemployed or retired. There is little local employment (School Teachers, Farming, Mining) except by travelling to Huntly or Hamilton.

Getting Setup
I have completed the purchase of the land and taken care of all the book work. I paid cash, though I have had to use my credit card for a couple of things until I can sell my old van and free up some cash.

I have downsized my mobile home to a cheaper and smaller one to free up some cash to invest in my new property and to buy some of the necessities of life, like a solar panel.

I have advertised the old van online and in magazines but still no results as yet. But it is now spring so maybe I will sell the van soon.

At the suggestion of one of my lady friends I am going to call my place "Tawhiti Rua". Tawhiti means far away and rua means two.

Background;
I was Secretary and Treasurer for Tawhiti Blocks (5000 acres of unproductive Maori land) in Tokomaru Bay during the 1980s. I see doing a Google there is a town in Taranaki called Tawhiti. So I see Tawhiti Blocks as tahi or number one and my place as number two or rua.

My New Van;
1991 Ford Econovan
FYU 11

Facilities in van;
46l fresh water
fridge
led lights
waste water
sink and bench
hot water
heater
230v certified

20l porti potti toilet
double bed
2 burner LPG gas cooker
small solar panel to charge battery
Outside awning
twin berth

I need to get;
400w inverter
2000w inverter
rust in rear removed
waste water tank
tool box door
solar panel 180w
195ah battery
12v regulator
microwave
fishing rod holder

I find the amount of water and the size of the toilet is enough to last me about two three weeks and maybe a bit more.

There are facilities in nearly all towns to empty the grey and black water and to take on fresh water and supplies.

I have been living on the road for many years. I had some brief periods at my Nieces and I occasionally stay at the local camp ground particularly to have a shower and to do some laundry.

After a bit of mucking around I finally have my address and mail sorted. The funny thing is the mail people drive past my place twice a day but I have to go to the next village (Pukemiro) to collect my mail as that is were they have a spare Post Box.

Ring me on 021-233-5427 before you leave to make sure I am there.
Sorry there is no cell phone coverage at Glen Afton

Glen Afton is an old mining town.
Nowadays there are a few houses a dairy and a club, but otherwise not much.

Kia Ora and Welcome.

Bill

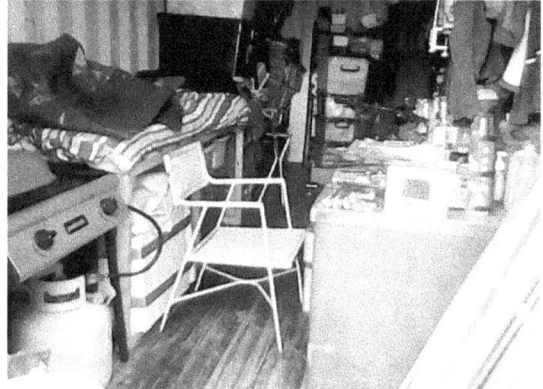

My place at Glen Afton in December 2011   Inside Container.

New Zealand Motor Caravan Association

Www.nzmca.org.nz

I am a member of the association and get a few benefits like a discount on petrol I purchase.

They also have or provide;
- → A good monthly magazine
- → A Certified Self Containment service
- → An excellent annual travel map and location of camping facilities
- → Provide several camp grounds the association owns
- → Provide Park Over Properties at no or a small cost at members properties
- → Monthly gatherings at some interesting places (I have not been able to attend of late as I work weekends, but I enjoy them when I can get to them)
- → A link with the Australian Association
- → Provide emergency drivers in the case of illness or accident
- → Provide a group insurance cover for vans which includes contents
- → There is an annual Motor Home and Caravan Show were several hundred vans gather
- → An annual conference and gathering
- → Mail Drop
- → Many online resources
- → A lot of members have excellent knowledge about motor homes and camping

Things I need to get or to check out

Slug gun and ammunition

Pine Trees felled
Get Solar panel and battery
Insurance for section!
In two years look at a small house or a double garage for a home or a second hand caravan.
Timber and a door for the container
Get my stuff from my secure storage and then cancel to save round $1000 per year.
Water Tank
check out weed eater
Cell phone coverage improved
check out motor scooter

Wild Food and Game

I am an experienced hunter gather, well a little bit, as I have lived with communities were living off the land and the sea is their normal way of life.

There are many wild plants and some wild game.

Puha
Water Cress
Rabbit
Fish
Muscles
Sea Urchins Kina
Abalone or Paua
Sea Snails or Bubus
Duck

Were I am there is land and quite a few lakes and some rivers, which have fish in them. Mostly the fish are not supposed to be there. We have Rudd, Carp, Cat Fish and Bream. Also there are some Trout. For Trout you need a licence, but not for the nuisance fish.

I read Rudd and Bream are edible but Cat Fish are real muddy. The other problem is that most of the lakes are polluted, mostly from farming run off and the fish will be polluted too.

In the creeks there maybe eels. I guess that fish from the rivers or creeks might be OK to eat.

I am about 60km from the sea (Raglan or Kawhia), but I guess I could go and do some fishing for awhile.

That leaves other things like rabbits and I do hear some turkeys running around. The turkeys I am not sure how wild they are but I hear them in different places so guess they are wild.

We do have wild rabbits in New Zealand though they are an introduced pest. I have not seen any yet so will wait and see.

I have had a quick walk around the immediate vicinity but have not seen any puha or water cress.

We also have wild deer and pigs, but I doubt if there are many round were I am.

I have been thinking about buying a slug gun and see what I can get with that.

Part of Wild Food Gathering is knowing what you are looking for and also not poisoning yourself.

I know some things like mushrooms when I see them and in NZ we do not have that many deadly wild foods or wild animals.

We do not have snakes, bears, lions etc. So going bush in NZ is OK just be careful of the weather and take some clothes and food.

I have always said that if I was lost in the bush I would not go hungry. It is a matter of using your head and not just heading for the nearest KFC or McDonalds.

I have a good sense of direction, though once I did get disoriented on a mountain climb, I was also tired from climbing and had been left behind by the group, despite my telling the leader she needed to keep an eye on the slower people like me. They eventual sent someone down from the hut on the summit to get me before dark.

Also when you live in a rural area and want to eat cheap, you need to be prepared to give some strange food a go.

Personally I love Tripe (sheep stomach), Sweet breads (sheep brains) and of cause mountain oysters (sheep balls).

I also love rotten corn with cream and sugar, smells horrible but tastes yummy.

So you need to get out of the KFC/McD way of life and give some new foods a whirl.

Plucking Ducks/Geese

To pluck a duck is easy, you do not pluck it LOL.

Just put the duck on its back and cut down the centre of the duck and peel back the feathers and skin.

Remove the two breast meats and then check to see if the legs are worth removing.

If the legs are worth removing then cut them off and skin the legs.

Job Done!!!!!!!!!!!!!!!!!!!

I usually just dice the duck meat and then make them into a stir fry with plenty of sauce like Worcester or soy sauce.

Do not tell people what they are eating and everyone will enjoy it.

Garden

I plan to have a good garden of vegetables and fruit and hopefully some nuts.

I have cut right down on eating meat and now just love some potatoes and vegetables or rice or pasta and vegetables.

I have in the past used brought vegetables or tinned tomatoes and vegetables. But hopefully I can now use fresh vegetables from my own garden.

Were I am is moderate weather, in the summer it will be quite dry and in the winter mild with a few frosts but no snow.

I have a creek on my property and a large drain across the road so water for the garden and trees should not be a problem.

Vegetables

Below are some of the vegetables I plan to plant. I have several large pots under a tree to protect from frosts and have planted some seeds to get things going. I have also have some strawberries in pots.

lettuce
silver beet
carrots
cauliflower
tomato
broccoli
peas
cabbage
beans

"Fast" Compost Recipe

This method can produce compost in a couple of months or less but is labour-intensive and requires frequent turning. Start your pile with a layer of browns, and then add a layer of greens. If the greens are not fresh, sprinkle in some blood meal or cotton seed meal, poultry manure, or other nitrogen source. Mix well and add water if necessary to moisten. Adding a layer of garden soil, old compost or manure to each brown-green layer will introduce more critters to speed up the process.

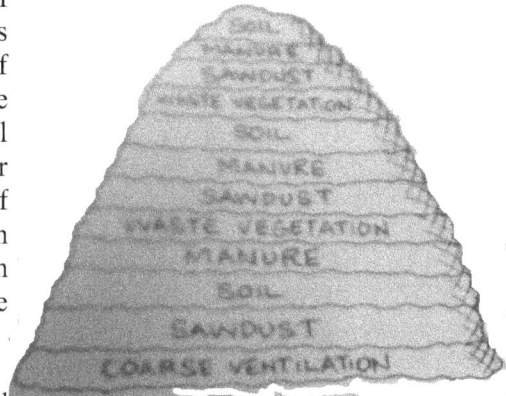

Continue adding and mixing layers of greens and browns until you either fill the bin or run out of materials. Slant the top of the pile to the centre to catch rainfall. You may want to cover the pile with a plastic covering or tarpaulin to regulate the amount of moisture entering your pile. The cover should not rest on the pile because it may cut off oxygen.

Periodically, check the moisture content of your pile. The compost should feel damp. Check the interior temperature of your pile and when the temperature reaches 140 degrees F or begins to fall, it is time to turn the pile. You will need to turn your pile every three to five days. Once your turning causes no rise in temperature, and the material appears dark and crumbly, your compost is ready.

Herb Garden

I have scored the inside of a washing machine which will be my herb garden.

I will plant some basic herbs like parsley, mint, coriander etc. As herbs are good for flavour but are also good for medicinal purposes.

Culinary Herbs

Culinary herb gardens are planned around the herbs that the cook uses the most. Depending on the style of the cuisine that comes out of the kitchen, the top choices for this type of garden can vary greatly.

The most popular cooking herbs include rosemary, chives, basil, oregano, parsley, thyme and sage. Mint is an herb that is widely used, but it should never be planted directly into the herb garden. Plant the mint in a container because it is invasive and could soon choke out the other herbs.

Medicinal Herbs

A single herb has properties that can ease an array of symptoms, so a medicinal herb garden doesn't have to be huge to offer relief for the occasional minor discomfort. Chamomile is a favourite because of its relaxing properties and because the subtle flavouring makes a good, basic tea to combine with other herbs. Echinacea, or coneflower, boosts the immune system and is used to treat inflammation.

Aromatic Herbs

Thyme, rosemary, mint, lavender and scented geranium are favourites of gardeners who choose to plant an herb garden based on fragrance. The aromatic properties of these plants can give pleasure whether cuttings are dried or used fresh. Dried, they can be used in potpourris or sachets to scent the wardrobe. The oils of these aromatic plants can be extracted from fresh cuttings if they are allowed to soak in carrier oils.

Herb descriptions

Angelica: A very tall biennial with large clusters of small greenish flowers. The main use is for a condiment or confection. Hollow stems may be candied. Roots and leaves are collected in late summer of second year of growth.

Anise: A dainty annual that has finely cut, serrated leaves with very small, whitish flowers in flat clusters. Leaves and seeds have a sweet taste that suggests licorice.

Basil: An annual that has light green or dark purple leaves. A number of varieties with different growth habits are available. Flowers are small, white and appear in spikes. Spicy leaves have many uses.

Bay, sweet: Also called laurel. Bay is an evergreen tree used as a potted plant in cold climates. This plant produces the well-known bay leaf, which may be picked for use or dried at any time.

Borage: An annual with coarse, hairy leaves and attractive sky-blue, star-shaped flowers. Flowers and leaves give a cool, cucumber-like flavour to summer drinks. Attractive to bees.

Caraway: A biennial that flowers in flat, white clusters with very finely cut leaves like carrot leaves. Caraway seeds are aromatic and are used as an ingredient of liqueurs. Popular for cooking.

Catnip: A hardy perennial with leaves that are green on top and grey underneath. Flowers grow in purple spikes. It is used for tea and seasoning and is attractive to cats.

Chervil: An annual with lacy leaves like parsley but paler green. It has flat heads of white flowers and is used like parsley.

Chives: Small, onion-like plant in clumps that produces light purple flowers. Useful as an ornamental plant. Leaves provide onion like flavour.

Cicely, sweet: Decorative fern like downy leaves. White flowers in umbels. Needs partial shade. Seeds are picked green and used fresh with other herbs. Leaves may be picked for use at any time. Once used as a sugar substitute and a furniture polish.

Comfrey: A very coarse perennial plant with prickly hairs on the leaves. Flowers may be yellowish white or pink in drooping clusters. Leaves large and somewhat bitter.

Coriander: An annual with umbels of pinkish-white flowers and feathery leaves. Leaves have a somewhat disagreeable odour. Seeds are widely used in spice mixtures and curry powders. Seeds may be used whole or crushed.

Dill: An annual with dark green stems and feathery bluish-green leaves. Flowers are yellow in flat umbels. Chopped leaves and seeds have many uses.

Fennel: There are several species, but sweet fennel is considered most desirable. Leaves are bright green and delicate below umbels of yellow flowers. It has a faint anise fragrance. Traditionally used with fish, but now has many uses.

Horehound: A coarse perennial covered with whitish hairs. Leaves are crinkled. Leaves and small stems should be cut before flowering begins. Most popular use is to flavour candy.

Hyssop: A hardy perennial with small, pointed leaves, spikes of blue flowers and woody stems. Harvest only youngest leaves, which may be added to salads. Flavour is slightly bitter and minty. Used to flavour liqueurs and sometimes as a condiment.

Lavender: Several different species may be grown, but the English lavender is considered the finest. Plants are bushy with narrow greyish-green leaves. Flowers are bluish purple in spikes. All parts of the plant contain the scent, but it is strongest in the flowers. Much used in potpourri and sachets. Also used for tea.

Lemon balm: Perennial plant with light green, heart-shaped leaves that are deeply veined. Yellowish-white flowers appear throughout the summer. May be harvested several times during the season, but first harvest is considered best. Many uses, but frequently added to jams, jellies and fruit salads.

Lemon verbena: Nonhardy, woody shrub for pots and indoor use. Long, pointed, dark green leaves come from each stem node in groups of three leaves. Lemon verbena adds a lemony taste to teas, cold drinks and jellies.

Lovage: A tall perennial plant with shiny, dark green leaves. Has hollow stems that terminate in clusters of yellow flowers. Leaves, young stems and roots are eaten. It gives a slightly spicy taste to many dishes or soups.

Marjoram, sweet: There are three major species, one of which is sometimes called oregano. Sweet marjoram is used as an annual plant often with thyme. It is sweet and spicy. Plants are low growing with small, grey-green leaves on tough, woody stems. Flower heads have small, pale mauve to white flowers. The delicate flavour is most used for beef, game or poultry.

Myrtle: The true myrtle is a non-hardy evergreen shrub with small evergreen leaves and small, creamy-white flowers that produce blue-black berries. Use as a pot or tub plant. Will take shearing well. Leaves used in potpourri and herb sachets.

Oregano: A sprawling plant with leaves much coarser than sweet marjoram. Although called oregano, there is some disagreement as to the best source of the oregano flavour. Among other plants with an oregano flavour, Spanish thyme, Thymus nummularius, is an alternative.

Parsley: A biennial plant with often curly, dark green foliage. Seeds are slow to germinate. Well known and the most popular of all herbs.

Peppermint: A spreading plant with numerous upright shoots that may reach a height of 2 feet. Dark green leaves are produced from reddish stems. Grows best in moist soils. Best cut just as flowering begins.

Rosemary: May grow outdoors for summer, but not winter-hardy outdoors. Needs sunny location and well-drained soil. Can be pruned severely if necessary to keep in proportion with pot size. Popular for veal, lamb, shellfish and other meats.

Sage: A woody plant with oblong leaves that have a woolly, grey-green covering that is lighter on the bottom. May grow 2 feet high but tends to sprawl. Several forms are available, including purple-leaved, variegated-leaved and dwarf growing. Needs a sunny location and well-drained soil. Used with meats and dressings.

Sage, pineapple: Not reliably winter-hardy and should be over-wintered in pots. Has rough, pointed leaves and attractive cardinal red flowers. Used to give a pineapple scent to potpourris or to add flavour to drinks such as iced tea.

Savory, summer: Produces small, bronze-green leaves and small white or lavender flowers. The small leaves are less conspicuous than the stems. Cut when in bud and hang to dry. Used as a condiment for meats and vegetables.

Savory, winter: This woody plant has shiny, pointed, dark green leaves and small white or lavender flowers. Needs a well-drained, sandy soil. Dead branches should be trimmed out. May be picked and dried at any time.

Spearmint: Has slightly crinkled leaves lighter green than peppermint. Needs moist soil, but very hardy. Leaves and stems may be picked anytime. For drying, pick stems as flowering begins. Leaves used in cold drinks or to make mint sauce.

Tarragon: Has somewhat twisted, narrow, dark green leaves. Grows best in partial shade. Fairly hardy, but needs winter protection to ensure survival in colder climates. Leaves and stems are used fresh to flavour vinegar. Flavour is lost during drying.

Thyme: Stems are low-growing, wiry and woody. Leaves are small and usually grey-green. Needs bright light and well-drained soil. Plants are not long-lived and may need replacement every few years. Other forms of thyme are also useful and attractive. Mother-of-thyme is a prostrate-growing species only a few inches in height. Lemon thyme is also popular. All thyme species may be used for seasoning food. Shoots should be harvested while in flower.

Woodruff, sweet: A low-growing perennial with shiny leaves in whorls around each stem. Should be grown in shady, woodland sites for best growth. Remove leaves just as the herb comes into flower or during flowering. Has been used for potpourri or strewn in storage cupboards and among linen. Used for the May cup or May wine. Best flavour occurs after leaves have wilted slightly.

Neighbourhood

The neighbourhood were I live seems OK so far. There is a local dairy for milk bread etc., where the prices are reasonable and a club rooms in the village.

Many local people have either spoken to me or waved and tooted out. I do not expect much trouble, there is bound to be the odd idiot hanging around the place but I plan to keep my head down and do my thing without annoying the locals too much, I hope!

I live on a main road (well sort of) there is some traffic either going to Huntly the nearest big town or to other villages like Glen Massey, Waingaro etc.

It is mostly sleepy villages and some farming and coal mining. Not much else is happening.

Most people would seem to be retired, unemployed or they work in bigger towns or cities.

Council and Planning Rules

Councils or Local Authorities how we love them, NOT.

In NZ as it is in a few countries you can do a certain amount without permits or paying any fees.

I can build a shed of 3mx3m or 10ftx10ft without a permit. I have also put a container on my property (6mx2.5m or 20ftx8ft). I can do most landscaping and gardening, build a fence or a small retaining wall without hassle.

Because I am in a rural community I can also do things with a permit and they are quite flexible.

There are some nice videos on youtube of 100 sq ft houses on trailers in the USA. They are great small homes.

Another reason for moving slowly is that as long as I do not have a proper home and not to many improvements my rates/property taxes are low. I pay rates of $93 per annum (plus a small regional rate). If I build a home I will be paying more like $500 per annum.

I get little for my rates not even a rubbish collection but that suits me fine.

I know with councils and bureaucrats you need to know your rights and quite a bit about the laws and regulations.

I have been studying the by-laws and the district plan that says what a land owner can and can not do and when a permit is required and how to get a permit and your project accepted.

I am following the by-laws as to what I can do and how far from boundaries I need to build etc.

I do not expect any problems for now, but you have to be on your guard. In a rural area like were I am the local council will generally turn a blind eye to a lot of things as long as no one complains, then they will act.

In a previous situation about 10 years ago, I was living in similar circumstances and someone complained twice. The local council came and had a look and then left as I was not doing anything illegal, despite the fact that I had five small buildings erected on the property.

Electricity, Alternative Energy

In the beginning I am just using the battery from my van for power. I have a 12v Cigarette Plug and a very small solar panel to top up the battery when the motor is not running.

I run my new radio, charge cellphones, use a small inverter to use my shaver, charge torch batteries, etc.

I am using my computer etc. at the library, at the local camp ground and extensively at work.

Once I get some more money and buy a solar panel I will have enough power for computer, microwave, kitchen whiz, etc.

The main thing is energy saving like using LED bulbs and turning stuff off you are not using. If you are used to not having much power it is easy to run your household on very little. You can spend a fortune on alternative energy. But I think it is far better to cut power use and the number of appliances. Things like an electric knife, or electric bread maker etc. are just not needed.

Going bush is a good time to de-clutter your life and get rid of all the junk you do not really need.

I do not own a TV or a flash stereo etc. I suppose in an ideal world it would be nice, But I do not consider these things add much to my life.

Happiness for me is the simply life, living off the land, meeting friends and real simple pleasures like a nice home made meal, or a BBQ and a couple of beers.

Solar Power

This will be my first option.

I will get one solar panel (180w), one battery (190ah), one regulator.

I will install it in the van for now and then see what happens latter on.

The cost will be about $1800.

I have about 12 years experience living on solar power. So I am quite used to wiring up 12v systems and running appliances through inverters. My only limitation at the moment is the lack of finances. Still I can make do with what I have got for now and better times are on the way.

There will be massive breakthroughs in both Solar Panels and Batteries in the near future, but at the moment we are stuck with what is now quite old technology.

Hydro Power

I have had a good look online for DIY Micro Hydro Schemes.

Most seem to be quite big. I just want to use a car Alternator and a battery which would also be linked to a solar panel.

I need to look at the fall and flow of the creek that flows through my property and there is a large drain across the road as well.

It does not have to be a fantastic flow just ticking over and doing it 24 hours a day.

I have had a look at my two creeks and do not consider there is enough water or fall to think about micro-hydro at this stage.

Wind Power

Is an option again I would build a simple system powering a car alternator.

You can just use a 44 gallon (200lt) drum and cut it in half and join up and use a bike wheel as a base.

See online you can use steel or plastic drums.

The Savonious Rotor
Savonius turbines are one of the simplest turbines. Aerodynamically, they are drag-type devices, consisting of two or three scoops. Looking down on the rotor from above, a two-scoop machine would look like an "S" shape in cross section. Because of the curvature, the scoops experience less drag when moving against the wind than when moving with the wind. The differential drag causes the Savonius turbine to spin. Because they are drag-type devices, Savonius turbines extract much less of the wind's power than other similarly-sized lift-type turbines. Much of the swept area of a Savonius rotor may be near the ground, if it has a small mount without an extended post, making the overall energy extraction less effective due to the lower wind speeds found at lower heights.

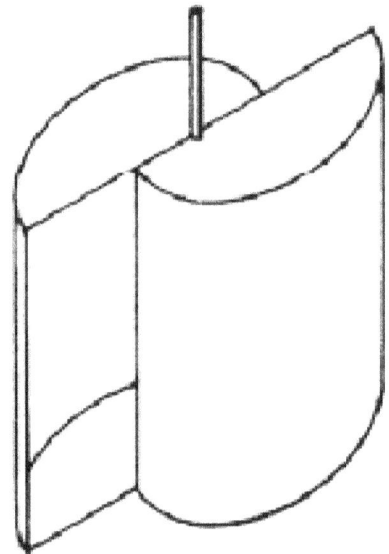

Vertical Axis Wind Machines From Oil Drums
http://en.wikipedia.org/wiki/Savonius_wind_turbine

Firewood, Coal, BBQ

I have a large pine tree on my property which will have to go as it restricts what I can do on the back half of my small section.

I have had some quotes of around $3000 to fell it, but that is a lot of money. At the moment I have other priorities.

So my plan for this year is to hire a chainsaw for a day and cut some of the low branches into firewood for next winter. I also called into the local open cast coal mine down the road the other day. You can by coal by the sack or by the trailer or truck load.

I will have some firewood and some coal. I have a brazier to burn the firewood and coal on. I will have to have it outside but it will be good for heating and cooking and as a BBQ in the summer.

Perhaps when I get a proper house I will get a proper indoor stove and maybe even a wet back for hot water.

It is nice in the winter to have a fire going and to have a pot of hot water on the stove. I can then have a hot drink, or some hot noodles or just fill a hot water bottle and go to bed.

I have also started to collect the pine cones from the large pine tree.. So that gives me a cheap heating for a few years.

If I do some of the work on the pine tree and I have decided to retain the bottom part of the trunk to make into a garden shed and a play house for my nephew, I should be able to get the rest cut down professionally at a cheaper price.

With alternative power supplies you always have several sources of power so if there is no sun or wind you have other options. So my options are Solar, Wood and Coal and then maybe Wind Turbine.

These should keep me going for awhile, I could also look at getting a petrol or diesel generator but that would be expensive to run. I could also just run the van and use that to recharge a battery etc.

Water Supply

I need a fresh water supply. In the beginning I am filling up my mobile home and some containers in town and bringing them home. This lasts about two weeks.

I will need to get a water tank and either build a house or put a roof on the container so I can catch the water.

I also have a creek flowing through my property and a large drain across the road. So water for the garden should be OK.

I have got used to not using much water. Townies use a large amount of water, but being a country boy I am used to saving and recycling water,

So I should be able to survive even if I have to use the creek water and look at purifying it. Which is something I should look into.

I also plan to have a dry toilet, i.e. one that does not flush with water. I have the brochure for one at round $3,000 which only needs to get rid of a bit of water (urine) and the solids are put onto the compost heap and recycled.

Food and Provisions

I am now able to buy in bulk as I have somewhere to store it, that is in my container.

cat food
pasta
rice
tinned fish
dates
coffee
sugar
biscuits
sultanas
potato
baked beans
spaghetti
nuts
flour
Tinned vegetables
Cornflakes
Rice Puffs
tooth paste
toilet paper
hand towels
rubbish bags
Soft Drinks
Bleach
vinegar
powdered milk

You need to rotate your supplies so they do not perish before they are used.

I plan to have some food on standby. Not too much just some bulk stuff like 5kg of rice and some toilet rolls etc. I do not think the end of the world is nigh, but hey it does not hurt to have some supplies on hand in case there is a natural or man made disaster that happens or if I get ill or run out of money.

Like at the moment we are in the middle of the Global Economic Meltdown and the USA and EU as well as the IMF and World Bank do not seem to have any answers and the status quo is certainly not an answer.

So like a good Boy Scout I am going to be prepared. BTW I have a copy of the Boy Scouts Survival Manual. It has some good stuff in it.

Basic Recipes

I believe in basic cooking and nothing too fancy, mind you my favourite meal is Fillet Mignon and Boysenberry Parfait. LOL

I have enclosed some simple recipes. I like creamed corn fritters or banana fritters, scones, muffins, rice risotto etc.

Nice and simple and easy to do with minimal ingredients.

Even if I had a million dollars I would still enjoy the simple things of life and some simple foods.

I have always liked cooking and eating. I used to help my mother when I was young. She did all home cooking of most everything, unfortunately nowadays it is so expensive to do say roast lamb and baked vegetables or biscuits. Still it is better than going to the shop all the time and if the shop is not there then it will be great to be organised to make some of the nice things of life to eat.

I will be cooking up a storm once I get organised at my new place,

I will not have an oven as such but a gas burner and the BBQ. I also have two convection cookers you can put on a gas ring or the brazier and cook a chicken, or a roast, or bake a cake, or about 6 muffins or scones at a time. You have to watch you do not burn the bottom of things and turning them over often helps keep them from burning.

I will also have a microwave when I get a solar panel, though you can not run it for too long.

Anyway here is a few simple recipes.

Classic Cornflakes

Ingredients
1 cup Cornflakes
1 dessert spoon sultanas or dates
1 kiwi fruit or apple

Method
Cut the kiwi fruit or apple into slices and then put them and the other ingredients into a dessert dish.

Serve with milk or cream.

Porridge

Ingredients
½ cup quick or instant oats/porridge
1 cup water/milk

Optional
diced apple
diced dates
sultanas

Method
Mix ingredients in a bowl.

Microwave 2 minutes, stir, microwave 1 more minute or till cooked.

Or in a saucepan heat till boils then simmer for 1 minute.

Serve with brown sugar, maple syrup or honey.

Scones

Ingredients
1 ½ cups self-raising Flour
¼ teaspoon salt
1 tablespoon butter or margarine
1 desert spoon sugar
2 tablespoons sultanas or other filling
½ cup Milk more or less to mix

1 egg

Could also be dates, cheese, chocolate (cocoa)

Method
Put flour and salt into mixing bowl. Add butter or margarine, cut into small pieces, and rub into flour until mixture looks like coarse breadcrumbs. Mix in sultanas or other filling.

Make a hollow centre of flour and mix in enough milk too make a fairly soft dough. Turn the mixture onto a lightly floured board and roll out gently until it is 2cm/ ¾" thick. Cut out into squares and place on a tray.

Microwave 2 minutes, turn the scones over and microwave again for approximately 2 minutes.

Or bake in a moderate oven for round 6-10 minutes till cooked.

Muffins

Ingredients
1 cup self-raising flour
1 egg
¼ cup water more less to mix
1 tablespoon sugar
2 tablespoons sultanas or dates
or 1 tablespoon cocoa
or do not add sugar or sultanas etc. but add

¼ teaspoon salt
½ cup cheese
some parsley
salt and pepper to taste

Method
Mix ingredients in a bowl. Stir as little as possible

Cook 3-5 minutes in Microwave

Omelette

Ingredients
3 eggs
salt and pepper to taste

Optional

Add Cheese, diced Ham, Mushrooms, Fish, etc.
Herbs/Parsley

Method
Beat eggs with fork or whisk in a bowl enough to blend yolks and whites thoroughly. Add salt and pepper and optional Filling.

Microwave in an Omelette Dish for 2-3 Minutes, turn over and Microwave 2 minutes.

Can also be cooked with oil in a fry pan.

Chocolate Bread Pudding

Ingredients
2 slices bread
2 tablespoons chocolate chips
½ cup milk
1 egg beaten
1 tablespoon sugar
½ teaspoon nutmeg/cinnamon/vanilla essence
2 tablespoons raisins or sultanas

Method
break up bread into an oven dish.

Mix other ingredients in a bowl and add to the dish.

Microwave for 3-4 minutes.

Or Bake for 20 minutes in moderate oven, more or less.

Pancakes

Ingredients

1 cup self-raising Flour
1 tablespoon sugar
1 egg
¼ cup milk
1 tablespoons butter, to cook with

Method
Serve with Maple Syrup or Honey.
put butter into a fry pan and heat.

Mix ingredients in a bowl, use enough milk to make a nice mixture.

Pour an amount into the fry pan and make a pancake. When bubbles appear or when it looks ready flip the Pancake.

Fudge Cake

Ingredients
1 tin condensed milk
1 cup mixed fruit
1 packet crushed wine (plain tea) Biscuits
1 cup desiccated coconut
1/4 cup nuts
2 tablespoons cocoa
1 teaspoon vanilla essence

Method
Place all dry ingredients into a bowl.

Add condensed milk and vanilla essence.

Mix well.

Press into a flat bowl/tray.

Cover with some desiccated coconut.

Pasta

Ingredients
1 cup pasta
½ teaspoon oil
pinch salt
water

Method
In a bowl, add pasta and water to cover.

Bring to boil then simmer till tender.
3-9 minutes depending on pasta type.

In microwave for 3-7 minutes depending on pasta type.

Rice

Ingredients
¼ cup rice
pinch salt
knob butter
water

Method
Rinse rice in cold water.

Add all ingredients to a bowl, using enough water to cover the rice.

Microwave on high for 3 minutes. Stir,

Microwave 5-6 minutes till tender.

Creamed Corn Fritters

Ingredients
1 medium can creamed sweet corn
1 egg
salt and pepper to taste
¾ cup self-raising Flour

oil or butter for frying

Can also be instead of creamed corn.
Small tin tuna/salmon, diced ham/luncheon, bananas.

Method
Combine sweet corn and egg in a bowl. Mix in flour and beat until smooth. Season with salt and pepper.

Heat sufficient oil and butter in a frying pan to lightly cover the base.

Drop in batter from a table spoon and cook until brown on both sides.

Drain on kitchen paper and serve immediately.

Rice Risotto

Ingredients
½ cup rice

some oil
1 onion sliced
1 carrot sliced
½ red pepper seeded and sliced
½ green pepper seeded and sliced
2-3 mushrooms
salt/pepper to taste
½ cup cooked meat or fish, Chicken, ham etc.

optional
2 tablespoons Worcester sauce or soya sauce
some wine
some mixed vegetables.

Method
The preparation for risotto requires more simmering than boiling and one must be gentle in the cooking process.

In a fry pan add ½ cup water and rice, heat gently till cooked, make sure to keep water added and stir frequently.

When cooked remove excess water. add some oil, soya sauce and other ingredients, cook till vegetables ready and heated through.

Batter, Sauces, Dressings

Fish Batter

Ingredients
1 tablespoon flour
1 egg
3 tablespoons milk
pinch of salt

Method
Mix in a bowl

Brown Sauce

Ingredients
1 tablespoon oil
1 onion chopped

1 tablespoon flour
1 cup water
1 teaspoon Marmite/tomato sauce

Method
Add oil into a fry pan, brown onion add flour brown lightly add water and Marmite/tomato sauce.

White Sauce

Ingredients
30g butter
4 tablespoons flour
1 cup milk
salt and pepper to taste
some lemon juice

can also add parsley, cheese, onion

Method
Add butter into a fry pan heat, add other ingredients and simmer till cooked.

Tartar Sauce

Ingredients
¼ cup Sour cream
½ cup Mayonnaise
2 gherkins, finely chopped
2 teaspoon lemon juice
1 tsp Lemon rind, finely grated
Combine all the ingredients, mix well and serve.

French Dressing

Ingredients
Method
pinch salt
pepper to taste
4 tablespoons vinegar
4 tablespoons olive oil

Method
Mix ingredient in a bowl. Whisk till combined.

Mayonnaise

Ingredients
1 egg
1 teaspoon mustard
½ teaspoon salt
¼ teaspoon freshly ground white pepper
1½ teaspoons white wine vinegar
1 cup oil, peanut or corn
1 to 2 tablespoons lemon juice

Method
Place everything but the oil and lemon juice in the Kitchen Whiz container. Process 10 seconds in the whiz. Add the oil, whiz 10 seconds and then taste.
Add lemon juice to your taste.

If the mayonnaise is too thick, thin with hot water or lemon juice. If too thin, process a little longer.

Chocolate Icing

Ingredients
50g softened butter or margarine
1 cup icing sugar
2 tablespoons cocoa powder
2 tablespoons boiling water

Method
Beat butter and icing sugar together in a bowl.

Add cocoa and boiling water and beat until creamy.

Make rather thick for pouring onto cakes etc.

Lemon Icing

Ingredients
1 cup icing sugar
1 table spoon lemon juice

Method
Place icing sugar in heat proof bowl, add lemon juice. Stand over a pan of hot water until the mixture is smooth.

Pour quickly over the cake and if necessary spread with a knife dipped in hot water.

Damper (Bread)

Ingredients
4 cups self-raising flour
1 teaspoon salt
30g 1oz butter
1 cup milk
½ cup water more or less

Method
Put flour and salt into large mixing bowl and rub in butter. Make a well in flour and pour in milk and water. Mix with a knife until the dough leaves the side of the bowl. Place on a greased scone tray and pat out until 20cm 8in in diameter.

Cut across on top and place in hot oven 220C 425F and bake for 25 minutes, lower heat to moderate 180C 250F and bake for a further 10-15 minutes or until the damper sound hollow when rapped with your knuckles.

Serve sliced with butter and golden syrup or jam.

Easy Bread

Ingredients
1 cup self-raising flour
1 egg
½ cup milk (enough to make mixture)
½ teaspoon salt
¼ teaspoon baking soda

Method
Mix the ingredients in a bowl.

Allow to sit for 10 minutes.

Heat a fry pan with a small amount of oil in it.

Add mixture and spread out to cover the bottom of the pan.

When it is cooked underneath, flip with an egg slice and leave till other side cooked.

Serve with butter and jam.

Simple Menu Ideas

Sausages eggs tomato chips
Fish eggs tomato chips
Steak eggs tomato chips
Rice Salmon fish sausages stew
Pasta Peas sardines/mackerel
Potatoes peas fish/stew/sausages
Fruit salad rice pudding
Porridge or wheat biscuits
Instant pudding and fruit
Pikelets
Scones
Fish cakes
Toasted sandwiches with baked beans, spaghetti, sweet corn, eggs, cheese onion pineapple
Sandwiches fish/cheese/eggs
Poached eggs with fish/sardines
Sweet Corn fritters
Omelette cheese, fish, ham, mushrooms
French Toast
Pancakes with golden syrup or honey
Salad with ham/luncheon
Bacon and Eggs, Tomatoes, Chips, Onions
Baked Beans on Toast
Bread Pudding
Instant Popcorn
Bacon and Eggs
Frozen precooked meal cooked in microwave
Instant Noodles and toast

etc.

NOKI (Bohemian Flour Dumplings):
This is a kind of gnocchi. It's the Hungarian version and the spelling is a variant. They are very easy to make and quite delicious. Perfect with a plain tomato-marinara sauce made from REAL summer tomatoes (otherwise, use a good brand of canned, plum).

Ingredients:
6 medium potatoes, cooked and puréed
1 teaspoon salt
½ teaspoon pepper
1 small onion, minced
2 tablespoons minced parsley
¼ teaspoon nutmeg

2 eggs (do not beat)
1/3 cup semolina (Cream of Wheat)
½ cup milk
2 cups sifted all-purpose flour

METHOD:
Mix potatoes, salt, pepper, onion, parsley, nutmeg, eggs and semolina thoroughly. Add milk and sifted flour. Mix all ingredients well. Knead on floured board. Shape into rolls, the approximate size of a walnut (in shell). Drop in boiling salted water. Boil 20 to 25 minutes. Remove with a slotted spoon.

Note: You can also brown in butter and serve with your favourite sauce or gravy.

Irish Soda Bread
2 cups wheat flour
1 tsp. baking soda
½ tsp. cream of tartar
½ tsp. salt
1 tbsp. butter
¾ cup buttermilk

Substitution: 2 tsp. baking powder can be used to replace both the baking soda and the cream of tartar.

Preparation: Mix flour, baking soda, tartar, and salt in a bowl. Mix in the butter. Pour in the buttermilk and mix quickly and lightly to a soft dough. Put on a floured baking sheet. Shape into a round loaf (do NOT knead the dough). Cut an "X" one-half inch deep across the entire top of the loaf with a sharp knife. Sprinkle lightly with flour.

Cook: Bake in preheated 450F oven 10 minutes. Then reduce to 400F and bake another 10 minutes. Cool on a wire rack.

Camp Biscuits or Biscuit Twists
½ cup flour
¼ tsp. baking powder
¼ tsp. salt
2 tbsp. oil or shortening or lard
warm water

Preparation: Mix flour, baking powder, and salt. Mix in oil or shortening. Add just enough warm water to make a stiff dough.

Camp Biscuits Cook: Drop by spoonfuls onto greased tin. Bake until brown.

Biscuit Twists Cook: Mold dough into a ribbon about two-inches wide and thick as your little finger. Twist around a clean stick in a spiral fashion, and bake over hot coals near a camp-fire until done (similar to a roasted marshmallow).

Chocolate Crunch Bars
Serving Size : 6
½ C Honey
1/3 C Margarine
¼ C Cocoa Powder, Sweetened
1 C Rolled Oats
1 C Dry Milk

Blend together everything except the Rolled Oats to a stiff dough. 2. Knead in the Rolled Oats, or roll the shaped bars in Rolled Oats. Carob powder may be used also.

Date Bombs
1 C Dates chopped fine
½ C Walnut chopped fine
½ C Sultanas
½ C Coconut Flakes
2 Tsp Rum Or Brandy -- optional

Mix and mash ingredients until well blended.
Form into 1-inch balls and roll in coconut.

Rice Pudding
¼ Cup Rice
1 cup milk/water
¼ Cup sugar
½ teaspoon salt
1 teaspoon vanilla essence

Gentle boil then simmer till cooked
Serve with fruit and cream
Add Sultanas or Dates

Gourmet Pies
You can turn almost anything into a pie, you just need a couple of sheets of puff pastry and a filling. Look in the fridge for some leftover chicken, beef, mince, vegetables, etc.

If you do not have pie dishes, make small ones in a muffin tin. Lightly grease, use the rim of a glass to cut the pastry into rings.

Basic Pasta Sauce

2 onions
some garlic
2 carrots
sticks of celery
1 table spoon oil
knob of butter
800g tomatoes diced

Put all the vegetables except the tomatoes in a food processor and whiz till superfine.

Drizzle the oil into a saucepan and add knob of butter. Add the vegetable mixture and cook on low heat for a few minutes.

Add tomatoes, salt and pepper and simmer.

Serve over the top of cooked pasta and vegetables or a tasty salad.

Potato Cakes
2-3 cups mashed cooked potatoes
tin corned beef, smoked fish, salmon or whatever. Add mashed potatoes and mix all ingredients. Shape into patties, coat each with flour.

Heat a fry pan with a little oil and heat till brown each side.

You could add chives, curry powder etc.

Serve with vegetables.

Homemade Pizza
2 teaspoons dried yeast
1 tsp sugar
1 ½ cups warm water
3 cups plain flour
1 tsp salt
3 tablespoon oil
tomato paste
grated cheese
herbs
favourite toppings

Mix the yeast, sugar and warm water together and stand for five minutes in a warm place. Place flour, salt and oil in a large bowl. Make a well in the middle of the mixture and then add yeast mixture. Knead for five minutes on a floured board then place the dough in a greased bowl and cover with a plastic wrap. Stand in a warm spot for 45 minutes or until doubled in size.

Now prepare your toppings and put the oven onto 200C.

The sky is the limit for toppings, ham, cheese, pineapple, gherkins, onions etc.

Divide your dough into four balls and and roll out on a floured surface. Add your toppings, starting with tomato paste at the bottom and finishing with cheese.

Bake on a flat tray for 20-25 minutes.

Five-cup Loaf
1 C self raising flour
1 C brown sugar (½ C probably just as good)
1 C milk/water
1 C coconut
1 C Sultanas or dates, or mixed fruit, or chocolate chips.

Mix all ingredients and bake in a greased and lined tin at around 180C until golden brown.

Muesli Bars
1 ½ C toasted muesli
2 ½ C Rice Bubbles
½ coconut
¼ C nuts
some butter
½ C honey
½ C peanut butter
½ C raw sugar
½ C chocolate chips (optional)

Grease and line a shallow baking tray. Mix muesli, rice bubbles, coconut and nuts together in a bowl. Put your butter, honey, peanut butter and sugar in a small saucepan and stir over a low heat until melted. Ring to the boil, then reduce the heat and simmer without stirring for five minutes. Pour melted ingredients into the bowl of dry ingredients and stir well.

When cool add chocolate chips and stir.

Spread the mixture on the tray, cool and then cut into bars.

Friday Special
3 tablespoon flour
1 tablespoon butter
some oil
milk

1 tablespoon mustard
1/ teaspoon Worcester sauce
salt pepper
grated cheese
1 tin sardines

Make a white sauce with the flour, butter and oil, adding milk slowly then other ingredients. Stir well until cheese is melted and finally add the sardines.

Serve on toast with tomatoes.

Creamed Chicken
3 tablespoon flour
3 tablespoon melted butter
1 ½ C milk/water
salt and pepper
1-2 C cooked chicken

Add the flour to the melted butter and stir till smooth. Add milk gradually, then salt and pepper, and cook for ten minutes stirring constantly.

Stir in the chicken and heat through. Serve with bread rolls.

Roast Duck
1 duck
2 sour apples, peeled, cored and chopped
125g breadcrumbs
some peas
1 tablespoon buttermilk1 onion, finely chopped
½ tablespoon mint chopped
salt pepper
dripping

Prepare duck for roasting. Make a stuffing from the apples, breadcrumbs, peas, butter, onion, mint, herbs and salt and pepper. Mix well and stuff into the duck.

Place in a brown paper bag and into a roasting dish with some dripping and water and bake at 200C for 2 hours or until cooked.

Curried Rabbit
1 rabbit, jointed
½ teaspoon ground ginger
30g flour
2 onions, chopped

2 sour apples, chopped
30g bacon fat or butter
1 teaspoon salt
1 tablespoon curry powder
1 ½ C vegetable stock
coconut milk
½ C grated coconut

Rub the rabbit with ginger and flour. Fry the onions and apples in fat until golden. Add the rabbit, seasoning and curry powder. Stir well and add the stock and coconut milk.

Simmer for approximately 1 ½ hours.

Fish Salad
250g cooked flaked fish
lettuce leaves
1 C shredded cabbage
3 celery stalks, chopped
¼ C salad dressing
¼ C chopped nuts
1 tablespoon chopped parsley

Place the fish on lettuce leaves. Combine the cabbage, celery and dressing and pile on top of the fish. Sprinkle with nuts and parsley.

Flaky Pastry
2 C flour
pinch salt
175g butter
½ C iced water

Stir the flour and salt together and rub in 25g of butter. Stir in the water gradually, roll dough lightly into long narrow strip, keeping sides straight and even thickness. Divide butter into three portions, put a third in small knobs, even distance apart, over two thirds of pastry and fold dough into three, un-buttered end first. Press edges and centre lightly with rolling-pin and give pastry a half-turn to left. Roll out again put a third of butter as before and fold again. Roll, use remaining butter as before, and fold once again, and pastry is ready.

Use for meat pies, sausage rolls or fancy pastries.

Puff Pastry
1 C flour
pinch salt
250g butter

lemon juice
cold water

Mix flour and salt and rub in a small knob of butter. Add lemon juice and enough water to make a soft dough. Lightly knead smooth. Make butter into an oblong shape and place on half the rolled out pastry. Fold other half over and seal edges. Turn pastry so that the fold is to the right and repeat the rolling, folding, turning and cooling until it has been done six times. Cook at 220C until lightly browned.

Suitable for jam puffs, oyster patties, vanilla slice etc.

Chocolate Coconut Biscuits
125g butter
¾ C sugar
1 C coconut
¼ C flour
1 egg, beaten
1 tablespoon cocoa
60g walnuts, chopped
pinch salt
few drops vanilla essence

Mix all ingredients in the order given and put into small teaspoon lots on a cool baking tray. Bake for 15 minutes at 180C. When cool ice with chocolate and decorate with walnuts.

Hokey Pokey Biscuits
125g butter
1 C sugar
1 tablespoon milk
1 tablespoon golden syrup
1 teaspoon baking soda
1 C flour
pinch salt

Cream together the butter and sugar. Warm the milk and syrup, stir in the soda until it foams, then add the butter and sugar. Beat in the flour and salt and mix well. Roll into small balls, place on a cold tray, press with fork   and bake for ten minutes at 180C. Makes approximately 40 biscuits.

Ginger Beer
500g sugar
1 level tablespoon ground ginger
1 teaspoon tartaric acid
1 teaspoon cream of tartar

5L cold water

Mix all the ingredients and add to the cold water, stirring until everything is dissolved. Keep in earthenware container till used.

Apple Cider
apples
boiling water
brown sugar

Cover any quantity of apple skins, cores and flesh with boiling water and stand in a warm place for three days when it will start frothing. A little brown sugar added improves the flavour.

Strain through a cheesecloth. Leave for another three days, strain again and then bottle in strong bottles. Tie corks down and leave for two days when it is ready to drink.

Lemon Honey
100g butter
350g sugar
rind and juice of three lemons
four whole eggs or eight yolks, beaten

Put the butter, sugar, finely chopped lemon rind and lemon juice in the top half of a double boiler and heat over hot water. Stir until butter is melted and the sugar dissolved. Stir in the beaten eggs. Continue stirring until the curd thickens. Pour into clean jars, cover and seal while hot.

Plum Jam
1.5kg plums
1.5kg sugar
½ L water

Boil together all the ingredients until a rich colour and sets. Bottle and seal while hot.

You could use a lot of fruit or berries to make this jam.

Apricot Balls
¾ C dried apricots, minced
1 C desiccated coconut
¼ C sweetened condensed milk

Mix all the ingredients together blending well to get a firm mixture. Shape into small balls and roll in coconut. Leave in a cool place until firm.

Snow Drop Rumbles

Ingredients
1 Cup icing sugar
½ Cup sultanas
½ Cup butter/margarine
1 Cup coconut + a little extra to sprinkle on Rumbles
3 tablespoons cocoa

Optional
shot of Rum.

Method
Melt butter and combined ingredients. Roll into balls in extra coconut.

Add a little water if still too dry.
Easy on the water.

Fruit Cream

Ingredients
¾ cup milk
2 teaspoons sugar
1 teaspoons cornflour
1 egg
1 cup fruit (kiwi fruit, berries, banana)
½ tsp vanilla essence
Cream for topping

Method
combine milk - cornflour – sugar in a saucepan. Cook over medium heat

Whisk egg. Gradually whisk into milk mixture.

Fold fruit into custard.

Add Cream for topping.

Healthy Muesli Balls

Ingredients
4 tablespoons peanut butter
½ cup milk powder
¼ cup of dates

¼ cup of sultanas
¼ cup of nuts
1 tablespoon honey
desiccated coconut for rolling balls in.

Method
Mix all the ingredients in a bowl, may need a dash of water to mix well.

Roll into small balls, covering in desiccated coconut.

Healthy Breakfast Bars

Ingredients
½ cup dry instant oatmeal
2 tablespoons chocolate chips
1 tablespoon peanut butter
2 tablespoons sultanas
1 tablespoon honey
¼ cup milk powder
2 tablespoons of dates
1 tablespoon honey

some desiccated coconut for coating bars in
dash of water to mix

Method
Mix all the ingredients in a bowl, may need a dash of water to mix well.

Form into a square in a tray or on a board, cut into bars covering in desiccated coconut or icing sugar.

Toasted Sandwich

Ingredients
4 slices bread
2 eggs
grated cheese
margarine

Optional:
Chopped tomato, onion, pineapple, bacon or tuna.

Can also use baked beans, spaghetti, creamed corn etc.

Method
Butter the bread.
Press the buttered side down into The Sandwich Maker. (I use one that goes on top of the gas ring).

Crack the eggs into the sandwich. Add as many optional ingredients as you want.

Put the next bread on top butter side up. Trim the bread from the edges.

Cook till golden brown each side.

Mega Sandwich

Ingredients
2 slices bread
¼ apple sliced
¼ onion sliced
½ cup diced or sliced ham, cooked chicken, beef or pork
1-2 tablespoons mayonnaise.

Method
Prepare ingredients and add on top of a slice of bread.

Add other slice of bread on top.

Thick Shake

Ingredients
splash milk
1 ½ cups vanilla ice-cream
chocolate syrup
Fruit blueberry, strawberry, banana
small chocolate bar – Mms

Method
Add ingredients to the Kitchen Whiz

Whiz till mixed.

Smoothie

Ingredients
Fruit - Banana - berries - Peach – Nectarine etc.
1 cup milk

dash vanilla essence
1 egg
1-2 tablespoons Milk Flavouring like Nestle Nesquik

To sweeten add 1 tablespoons honey or maple syrup.

Method
Break or cut up fruit, add to the Kitchen Whiz, add other ingredients.

Whiz till mixed smoothly.

BBQ Cooking

I have purchased an $89 BBQ, it is great and very handy, it runs on LPG gas. This is a great alternative to mains power or gas cooking. The gas bottle cost me $35 to fill and I know it will last me several months of cooking.

You can do heaps of things on a BBQ, like boil water for coffee/tea, soup, rice, pasta. You can bake potatoes, carrots, fish, meat etc. You can use a convection over on top of the BBQ to bake scones, muffins, cakes, biscuits, bread, meat, chicken etc.

Baked Potatoes
Peel some potatoes, sweet potatoes (Kumara), carrots etc. Cut into small pieces. Place on some tin foil and add some salt pepper, and a little oil. Wrap the parcels and place on the BBQ, turn often and bake.

Baked Fish
Follow the same as the Baked Potatoes, but add some lemon juice as well. Only bake a couple of minutes per side.

Meat
Beef, Pork, Chicken pieces can all be done well on a BBQ. With some of the meat you can marinate for a few hours in Worcestershire or soy sauce and some salt and pepper. Cook each side a few minutes according to taste.

Kebabs
These are tasty and easy to prepare and cook. On a skewer place small pieces of onion, meat, olives, peppers, cabbage, broccoli, etc.
Place on the BBQ and turn often.

Most of all have a few beers and enjoy the occasion and the food.

Grilled Corn on the Cob

Cooked in Aluminium foil

Remove the husks and the silk. Spread the corn generously with margarine or butter, salt and pepper. Wrap in heavy aluminium foil (double thick). Place over a medium heat on the grill about 6 inches from the heat source. Grill 15-20 minutes, turning often.
Cooked in the husk

Carefully fold the husk back and remove all the silk. Cover the ear with margarine or butter, salt and pepper. Fold the husks back in place and tie with heavy string that has been soaked in water. Place over a medium heat on the grill, about 6 inches from the heat source. Cook 20-25 minutes, turning often.
Corn is done when no milky juice leaks when kernel is cut or pricked.

Chicken satay skewers

You can prepare these chicken satay skewers ahead of time by marinating the chicken breast pieces in satay sauce for at least 30 minutes. Whether you choose to make your own satay sauce or use a sauce out of the bottle, these skewers are delicious and really simple to prepare.

Special Info:
Gluten free, Lactose free

Ingredients:
4 free-range chicken breast fillets (about 800g), cut into 2cm cubes
Zest and juice of one lemon
1 tablespoon olive oil
Homemade Satay sauce, or a jar of your favourite Satay sauce (I like Asia@home Thai Satay)
10 wooden or metal skewer

Method:
Combine chicken, lemon zest, juice and oil in a ceramic dish, cover with plastic wrap and place in fridge to marinate for at least 30 minutes.

If you are using wooden skewers, soak in water for the 30 minutes to prevent them burning under the grill.

Divide chicken into 10 equal serves and thread onto skewers.

Preheat BBQ to medium-high heat, cook skewers for 3 minutes, turn and then cook for a further 3 minutes or until chicken is cooked and starting to brown.

Heat satay sauce in a small saucepan or in the microwave.

Serve skewers drizzled with satay sauce or with the sauce in individual bowls on the side.

Barbecue Chicken and Peach Kebabs with Bacon

what you need
1/4 cup BarBQ Sauce
1 lb. (450 g) boneless skinless chicken breasts, cut into 16 pieces
2 peaches, peeled, each cut into 8 pieces
8 slices bacon, cut crosswise in half

make it

HEAT barbecue to medium-high heat. Reserve 2 Tbsp. barbecue sauce. Wrap each chicken piece with 1 bacon piece. Repeat with remaining chicken and bacon. Thread alternately with peach pieces onto 4 skewers. Brush with remaining barbecue sauce.

GRILL 12 to 14 min. or until chicken is done, brushing with reserved sauce the last 2 min.

NOTE If using wooden skewers, soak them in water 30 min. before using to prevent them from burning on the barbecue.

Hobbies and Crafts

I plan to use part of my container as a workshop and to practice some crafts.

The idea is to keep myself amused and to have some skills and to have some goods to sell or trade if the SHTF. But even so I could be growing vegetables and fruit and some crafts and go to the markets and make some pocket money.

Pyrography or wood burning

is something I would love to get into.

I love wood and natural products and I could marry it with my other craft of photography and make some wooden postcards.

My other love is computers and I will use them to write books and market them online and through friends and contacts.

Photography I have been doing most of my life. I have photos from way back and try and take heaps when on holiday etc.

I have in the past sold postcards etc. so maybe it is time I tried that again.

My garden will be a hobby too and maybe I will have plenty of vegetables and fruit to trade or sell.

I also make a bit of money from online books and ebooks.

I keep a needle or two and some thread, because I guess if there is a real major event you will have to make and mend stuff if the shops are closed or unreachable.

I have all my tools and could tackle a few problems with the gear that I have.

Wire Art

I would love to do some wire art in combination with Pyrography. I could make a pen and letter holder from wood and some wire. Or a picture holder using some of my own pictures.

I need to source some supplies. Which if TSHTF maybe difficult. Still it is worth a look at as will keep me busy and maybe provide some cash income or for barter.

Communications

Were I am living there is limited cell phone coverage at present. There is a underground copper cable connection about 400m away but it would not provide Internet Broadband as it is too far from the exchange (about a 8km limit for copper). It would also no doubt cost me quite a bit to get connected to a landline and then after pay at least $50 per month. More and more people are abandoning the idea of having a landline and are using other means of getting connected and communicating.

I will be able to run my cell phone, 7 inch Android Tablet or my Laptop as I will have Solar Power and some Mains Inverters.

I have been looking at alternatives.

Satellite Phone

They are available all round the world, they are reasonable priced to use at round $2+ a minute, but the phones cost $2300.00. Heard a person on the radio the other saying that when he travels he uses a sat phone and it cost him $800.

Cell Phone

In New Zealand we have the Government and private enterprise implementing a Rural Broadband Initiative as part of 1.5 billion dollar upgrade of the Internet to a much faster speed and more widely available.

In my region they are going to extend the landline network by laying and extending the fibre cable network and in the rural area were I am to install and additional 25 cell towers which will be connected to this fibre network.

However I am not aware were the actual towers will be and how long they will be in doing the upgrades.

I have an Android Smart Phone with Dual SIMs, this gives me good access to the phone and the internet. I also have a 3G USB Modem which is expensive but very handy in my Mobile Home, but of cause you need to have Cell Phone Coverage.

I also use the library and there free WIFI access and some hotspots at camp grounds or motels/hotels.

Rural WIFI

Several companies offer Rural Wifi, though it seems their coverage out my way is limited. Still I need to make some phone calls to find if they do cover my place.

Orcon charge $499 installation and $56 per month on a 24 month contract.

No8wireless charge $300 installation and $59 per month for 10gb on a 24 month contract.

Radio Telephone

When the guy delivered my container he made a call on his radio telephone. He had an actual phone connected to it and dialled a number and the person answered.

I know these are .meant for big business and large trucking companies, but I plan to look into the ins and outs of having one and the cost.

Satellite

This is an option as well, several companies offer a satellite service

Farmside offer a service, $300 Installation and $60 per month for 500mb of traffic on a 24 month contract.

Wireless Nation offer one as well for $200 installation and $70 per month for 1gb of traffic on a 24 month contract.

www.wirelessnation.co.nz
www.orcon.co.nz
www.farmside.co.nz
www.no8wireless.co.nz

So as can be seen there are many and varied options to get some telecommunications going as lest until TSHTF.

After all this research I went and spoke to a couple of people at the local school. They told me their broadband was terrible and real slow and would not get updated till 2015.

They also said that cell phone coverage is available on the hill on the outskirts of the village and in the middle of the village.

I went back to my place and low and behold I got a text message saying the had been a call on my cell phone. I walked into the middle of the village and got satisfactory coverage.

That inspired me to do some research on line about cell phone boosters. I found some stick on thingys solution or an internal and external aerial option, I also found a video about a cantenna (two cans soldered together and an aerial connection attached and attached to the phone. Ranging in price from $4 for stick on thingys to $250 for the external aerial.

So I went to my friendly trading site and ordered two cheap options and will see what difference they make. (They did not do much, seem mostly designed for older phones with aerials)

Next I have ordered a passive connector for my phone and try the cantenna idea, if not I will try a piece of wire or buy one of the aerials.

So that is positive and will make a big difference to my new lifestyle.

The good thing about getting cell phone coverage is that it is effective and fairly cheap. I have a total of 4 SIM cards and two cellphones (one for work) as well as my 3G USB Modem Stick. So this will give me good communications.

I am on prepay plans for my cellphones as I do not like being on 12/24month contracts. That is the big downside of most of the alternatives I looked at, they want a 24 month contract.

http://www.wisebread.com/no-signal-5-quick-ways-to-boost-your-cell-phone-reception-updated http://cellutronics.co.nz/House_Antenna_Kits.php

The Internet

Hopefully even if TSHTF we will still have the internet!

It is a fantastic way to keep in touch, to find and share information, to buy stuff, to check bank details and pay bills, and to keep abreast of world and local events.

I use;
Email leftfieldnz@gmail.com
Google Search
Google Maps
Skype
Facebook
Online Banking
Trademe

Other Options
I also use a 2degrees 3G USB Modem Stick which gives me WIFI via a Mobile SIM card. Or I use www.zenbu.net.nz outside a local motel or at the local camp ground and the library which has free WIFI.

I also use my smartphone for email, google maps and some web surfing.

Shortwave (World band) Radio

I have splashed out $45 and have brought a flash radio to keep in touch. As well as AM and FM for local stations I have 7 bands of Short Wave. BTW it also has a USB and SD Card slots to play MP3 music.

I have heard in English;
Radio Australia
Radio Republic of Iran
China Radio International
Family Radio (A USA Religious Station)
Vatican Radio
Voice of Russia

I would expect to find Radio New Zealand International, Voice of America, BBC, and other stations as well.

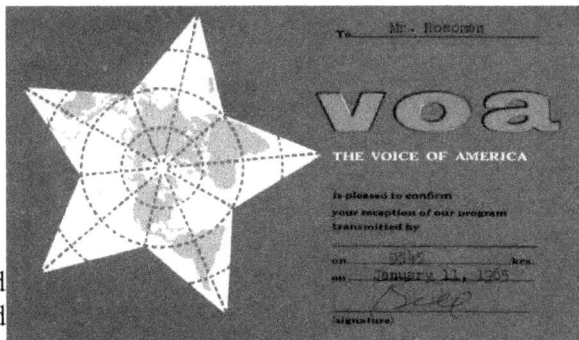

Of cause there are many other radio stations in other languages.

A major event maybe localised and the local radio stations maybe disabled or taken over by hostile forces so having Short Wave and access to overseas radio stations will be very handy especially if TSHTF.

But anyway it is nice to be able to listen to overseas alternatives. I have listened to short wave radio all my life so really enjoy it.

There is also utility stations like WWV, a station based in Boulder, Colorado, USA, providing frequency, time and weather information. On 15, 20 and 25mhz.

One of my QSL (reception) cards from the 1960s.

Listen to the higher bands 13, 15 to 17mhz during the day and the lower bands 7 to 12mhz during the night. An aerial is useful and any length of wire thrown out the window is good.

Frequencies change with the seasons and are also affected by the Sun Spot Cycle. But Shortwave Radio is great if the Internet and Phone lines go down in anyway. It is also free apart from buying the radio and having some power to run it. I have just connected two wires were the batteries go and plug it into a 12v plug with a 6v cut down voltage in my van and it works fine.

Interesting Web Sites

www.fema.gov /
www.ehow.co.uk/how_5101843_make-disaster-preparedness-kit.html
www.youtube.com/watch?v=SbRvsWuWNUM
Small House in USA
www.gonebush.org
www.gray-nomad.com
www.thegreynomads.com.au/
www.ledsunlimited.co.nz
www.odourbegone.co.nz
www.hobanz.co.nz
www.smarthomes.co.nz
www.legislation.govt.nz
www.lifestyleblock.co.nz
www.warnington.co.nz
www.wagenerstoves.co.nz
www.treecrops.org.nz
www.lewisgray.com
www.rd1.com

www.oasisclearwater.co.nz
www.ecotech.co.nz
www.kingsseeds.co.nz
www.powerspout.com
www.tradene.co.nz
www.healthline.govt.nz
www.zenbu.net.nz

To Check a vehicle ownership and any amounts owing on the vehicle
www.ppsr.govt.nz/cms/banner_template/CKEXAPP
SMS 3463 send registration number

Mail

I have a Rural Mail Delivery five days a week. If I hit the road I could get my mail from a Mail Drop Company or from the NZ Motor Caravan Club who offer the service.

Also
www.privatebox.co.nz
www.servcorp.co.nz

Barter or Trade

Heard a very good programme on the radio about Barter and Trade. It is alive and well in the 21st century.

Nowadays you can barter or trade locally with neighbours or at a local market and also globally with the internet and all the online opportunities that offers.

Www.ebay.com
www.trademe.co.nz
Www.freecycle.org
www.helpx.net /
www.wwoof.co.nz /
www.couchsurfing.org /
barter
green dollars
time bank
lets
batercard business
www.bartercard.co.nz /
www.tradetosave.co.nz /
www.barterzone.co.nz

www.swapster.co.nz

reciprocal trade
b to b
Farmers Market
Hamilton Farmers Market
http://goo.gl/9k4BI

Community Food Banks
Community Curtain Exchange
Garage/Boot Sales

A Comment on Barter
www.guide2.co.nz/money/guides/managing-money/is-it-smarter-to-barter/82/7343

Also crowd financing/micro lending/crowd sourcing is interesting.
This is were many individuals put in a small amount for projects that are real small or that traditional lending institutions like banks would not lend on.

They have a great success rate and worth looking into.

Transport

I have a Motor Home (RV) which runs on petrol, it costs me about $50 per week for petrol alone.

So that would not last long!

I also have a bicycle which maybe handy.

A motor bike or scooter would be handy and I may look at that down the road a bit.

I took the bus the other day it was quick, efficient and cheap. To travel from Hamilton to Huntly cost me $4, it is about 40km and in my van would cost at least $10 in petrol.

Community Resources

Community Resources are many and varied and a lot are free or low cost.

A Friday market is in Williams Street, Huntly and there is a farmers market in Hamilton, Cambridge and Pokeno. These can be a source for fresh and cheap local products and an outlet for your own crafts and produce.

Local Library

The local library has many resources.

They include;
Books, CDs, DVDs (a lot of which are free and some at a small cost)
Free internet and WIFI
Use of power (computer, cell phone)
toilet
heater
Local council resources and services
reference material
Advice
Meeting Friends
They are also going to make ebooks available.

Huntly (my nearest town)

food
petrol
RSA club (several clubs for social occasions)
mail and post shop
tyres
repairs like plumbers, electricians, mechanics etc.
Police, Fire, Ambulance, St John
Shopping
Community Groups
Community Centre
Library
Walks/Reserves/Parks etc.

Huntly Camp Ground

For $10 a night (non power site) I get;
Use of Kitchen and cooking and cleaning facilities
Use of TV
Laundry for a fee
Internet WIFI for a fee
Power to run computer, charge my cellphones in the kitchen
Fresh Water
Dump station for grey and black water (empty toilet)
Information on camping/motels and Travel information
Shower

Toilet
BBQ
Dump Rubbish
Etc.
Animals are allowed

So you can have fun and access facilities for little or no cost.

My nearest large city is Hamilton and here I can get a better selection of products and services and usually at better prices than I can locally.

However with the increase in petrol prices etc. you have to think twice about rushing into town on a whim.

Animals and Pets

Going outback and if TSHTF animals and pets will need feeding and looking after.

I have a cat, I find them good company, great for rodent control, good guard dogs. A dog maybe handy for protection and guard duties. Were I am there seems to be many dogs.

For animal food I would have to catch fish or rabbits or have chickens for food after the shop supplies run out.

Other animals like sheep, cattle, horses are not so bad as they mostly eat grass.

Animal health would be a problem as well, it pays to keep a close eye on your animals and tackle problems early.

You have to be prepared to make the hard choices when it comes to animals. Unfortunately you have to sometimes kill animals for food or if they are very ill, it is a fact of life.

I made the choice a long time ago, if I am to survive I occasionally have to make some hard decisions and I will, coping out is not an option.

Many years ago I attended a one day butchery course, I and my neighbour used to keep and feed a pig. We used to kill it and get it made into bacon and sausages etc. It was a great idea.

BTW reminds me we also had a communal water supply, were we all paid for a pump in the creek and the pipes to four houses in the locality.

I have cut right down on meat so would not keep many animals for food, plus I do not have much room anyway.

Some names for what I am doing

way outback
downsizer
gone bush
fringe dweller
gone feral
off grid
homesteader
downsizer
frugal
lifestyle
SHTF
survivalist
prepper
gone troppo

I really love to live in the country. Towns are OK but they are also a pain and getting very expensive.

In the country you can have a garden, trees and even wild foods.

So I do not mind going bush and enjoying life in the slow lane.

Organising Yourself and the Local Community

If TSHTF you will need to talk to your neighbours and local community.

Things like security, food, law and order, health, cooperation for building, sharing resources and food, trading and barter, would all be items to discuss and organise.

I would form a committee and some groups in charge of various aspects of survival and living in a civilised community.

I would also look at cooperation with other communities who have resources and food etc.

It would quickly come to the realisation that you could not rely on the local Police and Local Government.

I have been involved in a cyclone (Bola) and a hurricane (Bernie). So I have experience about being cut off from society and being self-sufficient for a week or more.

In both events there were a few deaths but mostly we survived very well and cooperated well.

We did have a lot of community resources and food etc. Many sheep, cattle and tons of sea food.

Radio Telephones were our main means of communications with the outside world, as the telephone exchanges did not last long when the power was off for many days. The telephone exchanges do have battery backup, but that did not last long.

We had a local Policeman, Fire Brigade and many construction men and vehicles. A hospital was 10km away though the road was blocked for a week. We also had a few helicopters buzzing around.

Hurricane Bernie flooding and damage from the sea.

I was a telephone lineman and had some extra equipment flown in by air force helicopter to assist me in getting the telephones back up and running.

I guess the biggest thing I have learned is that you need to be practical and organised and be able to work with a community in crisis.

A survival kit is of cause a brilliant idea. TSHTF event maybe man made like a financial meltdown, riots, military attacks, or it maybe a natural event like fire, earthquake or hurricane.

I do not have a survival kit as such, I do have lots of food and clothes etc. in my van and at my place in my container. I also have a bag packed with some basic clothes and stuff, which I could grab if you need to leave in a hurry.

I also have some bottled water to use.

You need to have enough food, water and basics like toilet paper, radio, batteries, matches, rubbish bags, clothes ready in case there is a major natural or man made event in your life.

Also get all your important documents and photos digitised and on a computer and backup in the cloud or somewhere.

Www.dropbox.com and www.zumodrive.com   offer 2gb of disk space free online.
Google Docs or your Gmail account are also good places to store valuable information.

It is to late when TSHTF to start worrying about supplies and looting the local shops etc.

Get organised and get a survival kit ready for the event you hope will never happen but just might, especially with global warming and some of the big disasters there have been happening around the globe of late.

Right now I reckon I could survive for several months with the food and other supplies or I have or have access to (like in the wild).

I always keep the van pretty well topped up and ready to hit the road. I have also been stocking up on supplies at home.

It seems to me that a lot of city dwellers have very little in the way of food and supplies and could come unstuck very quickly in the event of something happening.

Tokomaru Bay Hotel was hit by a large slip. It was demolished and rebuilt in 1988.

So be organised for the worst!

Keep your cool and tackle one problem at a time.

Do not Panic!

I have never been involved in or seen riots or military on the rampage, but can imagine the hurt and harm and community calamity it would cause.

So there are many reasons for being organised.

Alternative Products

- ➢ baking soda and vinegar for cleaner
- ➢ Water purifying add a little bleach
- ➢ Prevent mosquitoes add a teaspoon of kerosene into water tank and remove other stagnant water sources.
- ➢ Grow Chestnuts for flour, stock food, etc.
- ➢ Preserve or dry vegetables and fruit
- ➢ Preserve eggs (my mother used to wipe eggs with a grease/jelly so they can not breath)
- ➢ Fruit drying (sheet of glass on a box, facing north) called fruit leather. Keeps in a sealed glass jar for years. Use semi-ripe fruit
- ➢ Of cause fishing, hunting and wild food gathering
- ➢ Flax for rope, kits, hats, etc. They even used to make shoes from flax
- ➢ Hot Chilli Powder as an anti-septic

Green Environmental Ideas
- ✔ Bee Friendly plants, flowers and trees will increase your general pollination
- ✔ Companion Planting will save on sprays and plant damage
- ✔ Permaculture is a good idea
- ✔ Worm Farm is an easy idea to do
- ✔ Recycle and reuse all waste

Alternative to Tea and Coffee

Tea and Coffee are very popular around the world. But they are mostly imported and expensive.

Tea and Coffee have a large social place in a lot of cultures. So what to do if coffee and tea are not readily available.

To infuse flowers and leaves, place them in a clean, wide mouth jig, pour boiling water over them, stir gently and leave them to stand for a few minutes. Strain and serve.

Clover tea: Dry the flowers of red clover and infuse three teaspoons in half a litre of boiling water.

Chamomile tea: the sweet tasting brew from Chamomile tea has been used for many generations. This herbal treat can help aid digestion, stomach pain, and give one a good nights sleep.

Lemon grass tea: lemon grass tea is an herbal infusion that has a zesty, lemony, and refreshing taste. This herbal beverage also shows evidence of having antibacterial and antifungal properties.

Herbal green tea: herbal green tea is a beverage that takes the leaves of green tea and combines it with the flowers, leaves, and roots of other herbs enhancing the already great health benefits and taste. You could use no green tea and more Rose Petals,

Ginger tea: ginger has been used for ages by many cultures to fight colds as well as a cooking spice. Modern claims suggest ginger tea may help with migraines and arthritis.

Peppermint tea: one of my favourite herbals, this tea has a nice minty taste that when consumed helps with various stomach disorders, one of which is IBS (irritable bowel syndrome). Also, the flavour is not as overwhelming as folks may think.

Spearmint tea: another mint tea, spearmint like its cousin peppermint helps sooth and relax the stomach and bowel. However, unlike peppermint tea, I found spearmint to have more of a slightly sweeter taste. Very refreshing when drunk cold!

Marjoram tea: Pour half a litre of boiling water over one heaped teaspoon of fresh or dried leaves and infuse for a few minutes before straining and serving.

Rosemary tea: Pour half a litre of boiling water over one heaped teaspoon of fresh or dried leaves and infuse for a few minutes before straining and serving.

Thyme tea: Pour half a litre of boiling water over one heaped teaspoon of fresh or dried leaves and infuse for a few minutes before straining and serving.

Rose tea: Add a quarter of a litre of rose petals to a half litre of water, simmer gently for 10 minutes and strain before drinking.

http://en.wikipedia.org/wiki/Coffee_substitute
Grain coffee and other substitutes can be made by roasting or decocting various organic substances.

Some ingredients used include: almond, acorn, asparagus, malted barley, beechnut, beetroot, carrot, chicory root, corn, cottonseed, dandelion root (see dandelion coffee), fig, boiled-down molasses, okra seed, pea, persimmon seed, potato peel,[2] rye, sassafras pits, sweet potato, wheat bran.

The Native American tribes of what is now the Southeastern United States brewed a ceremonial drink containing caffeine, "asi", or the "black drink", from the roasted leaves and stems of the Yaupon Holly (Ilex vomitoria). European colonists adopted this beverage as a coffee-substitute, which they called "cassina".[3]

Ground roasted chicory root has been sold commercially on a large scale since around 1970, and it has become a mainstream product, both alone and mixed with real coffee. It was widely used during the American Civil War on both sides, and has long enjoyed popularity especially in New Orleans,

Dandelion Coffee : Roasted dandelion root, ready to be used to prepare dandelion coffee. Harvesting dandelion roots requires differentiating 'true' dandelions (Taraxacum spp.) from other yellow daisy-like flowers such as catsear and hawksbeard. True dandelions have a ground-level rosette of deep-toothed leaves and hollow straw-like stems. Large plants that are 3–4 years old, with taproots approximately 0.5 inch (13 mm) in diameter, are harvested for dandelion coffee. These taproots are similar in appearance to pale carrots.

After harvesting, the dandelion roots are dried, chopped, and roasted. They are then ground into granules which are steeped in boiling water to produce dandelion coffee. [5]

Dandelion coffee is said to be a good tonic for the liver.[6] A bitter tonic made from the dandelion root is also used as a laxative.[7]

Acorn Coffee: Pick some acorns, Chop the nuts roughly and roast them in a moderately hot oven. Cool and grind and return to a moderate oven until the ground nuts are well roasted. Place the required amount in a wide mouthed jug, pour boiling water over them, stir and leave to steep for ten minutes. Strain before drinking.

First Aid and Health

I hold a basic first aid certificate and always carry an extensive first aid kit.

I have been lucky in life and the only scare really was colon cancer some seven years ago.

My theory is if your numbers up then it is tough bickies.

But there again with some common sense and a bit of training you at least should be able to handle the basics of first aid.

Also you can make things better if you are not over weight, do not smoke and do not over do alcohol and have a healthy diet and some exercise.

Having a first aid book handy seems like a good idea and having a good first aid kit is entirely sensible.

Your health can be maintained by eating lots of fresh vegetables and eating some of the wonderful herbs we have available.

Western medicine tends to treat the symptoms like taking headache pill rather than addressing the cause of the headache. On headaches, all pain is in the mind, a bit of meditation and a healthy diet may help ease the pain. You also need to find out why there is pain, what is the cause of the pain.

I think you should have some basic medicines and some basic bandages etc.

Training on a first aid cause would also be a good idea. Having a good supply of any medication your family requires would be a great idea.

The caravan club says you should have a copy of your medical details attached to the inside of the cupboard under the sink in your mobile home so if your are ill or have an accident people will know some of your medical records and who your doctor is.

I do not take any medication, though my eyesight is getting worse. I have heard a guy on the radio offering natural medicine to relieve the symptoms for various diseases. He still believes in traditional western medicine, but that some natural medicine would not hurt as well. I live in a country and have seen the use of traditional medicine used by the indigenous Maori of New Zealand.

So you do not always need to rush off to the doctor, sometimes a little lie down and some nice herbs may be a great alternative.

I am interested in growing some herbs for their medicinal uses.

Gear you might need

Shovel
Spade
Hammer
Hand Saw
Nails and Screws
Gun and Ammunition
Fishing Rod and Reel
Ropes
Rubbish Bags
Spanners
Timber/Lumber
Tarpaulins
Electric Drill
Electric Skill Saw
Screwdrivers of various sorts
Socket set
Pipes of various sorts
Glues and sealants

Jig Saw
Hand Drill
Electric Sander
Paint and Stains
Planks and Plywood for emergency repairs
Fence Posts
Pliers and Side Cutters
Electrical wire and fittings including joiners
Tape of various sorts

Some Projects for Rural Living

Build a simply Cantenna

You need a drink can (Aluminium), a pair of tin
cutters (or side cutters), a pair of pliers.

Cut the top off the can
Cut down both sides of the can and remove half
the can side.
Bend of the edges of the cut can to tidy up and
make safe.

Using the pliers punch the bottom of the can to form a dip for the cell
phone to sit in.
Place the phone in the cantenna and point towards nearest cell tower.
Try different locations and heights.
Certainly worth a try.
You could try putting extra aluminium foil on the back of the can to
increase the size of the signal trap.

Another Cellphone booster
You need a salad bowl, some aluminium foil, some
packaging tape.

Cover the inside of the salad bowl with aluminium foil.
Tape the cellphone so it is suspended in the middle of the
bowl.
Point in the direction of the nearest cell tower.

Another Cantenna

You need;
2 steel cans
Solder and a soldering iron
Antenna Connector (BNC type female chassis (Bulkhead))
Pigtail Connector (one end BNC type the other is the same as the aerial port on your cell phone)
A short piece of copper wire (1 ¼" or 31mm)

Remove the lids and contents of the cans and clean them.
Remove the bottom of one can and then solder them together.
Measure 97mm from the bottom of the can and cut a hole for the antenna connector
Solder a short piece of copper wire into the antenna connector to act as the aerial
Fit the connector into the tin and solder into place.
Connect the pigtail to the can and the antenna port on the back of your cell phone (or use a passive connector if there is nor aerial port).
Point the cantenna towards the nearest cell tower.

http://binarywolf.com/249/coffee_can_antenna.htm

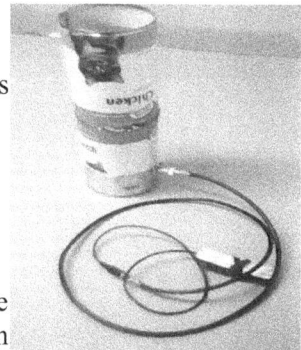

2 Degrees Mobile is multi band 900mhz 1800mhz and sometimes 2.5ghz

Coffee Can or Pringles Can?

This wi-fi antenna design is a much simpler DIY project than the pringles cantenna. Basically there are 3 parts to a build-your-own 2.4 Ghz cantenna kit: a pigtail, an N-female connector and a metal coffee can. A smooth metal can is better, because irregular surfaces, such as ribbed cans, can cause internal reflections and scatter radio-waves.

The coffee can antenna is a waveguide/feedhorn, which can be used by itself, or in combination with a parabolic dish for greater gain/distance.

Size and shape of a microwave waveguide (the coffee can) and the placement of the radiator inside the waveguide is important. The 5.25 inch/133mm long coffee can (4 inch/102mm diameter) antenna is made by following the steps below.

Step One
Drill a ½ inch/12mm or five-eights inch/16mm (depends on the N connector) hole in the side of the all metal can for the N connector. The position of the N connector hole is determined by the

overall diameter of the can. Measure up from the inside of the can.

4" diameter, hole is 1.72" from bottom
3.75" diameter, hole is 1.85" from bottom
3.5" diameter, hole is 2.07" from bottom
3.25" diameter, hole is 2.5" from bottom
3" diameter, hole is 3.75" from bottom
101.6mm diameter, hole is 43.7mm from bottom
95.25mm diameter, hole is 47mm from bottom
88.9mm diameter, hole is 52.6mm from bottom
82.6mm diameter, hole is 63.5mm from bottom
76.2mm diameter, hole is 95.25mm from bottom
If necessary, here are more measurements. Read more about wavelength calculations or a javascript 2.4 GHz directional antenna calculator or download a freeware calculator.

Step Two
Insert and solder a 1.2 inch/30.5mm piece of 12 gauge solid copper wire (1/4 guide wavelength size) into the N connector to serve as your driven element (radiator). A piece of brass rod will work as well. The wire side goes in the can. The other side, where the cable attaches, goes outside of the can.

N-Female chassis (panel) mount connector

Step Three
The N connector, one of the first connectors capable of carrying microwave-frequency signals, is a threaded RF connector used to join coaxial cables. Solder (preferred), epoxy glue or use screws to attach the N connector/element assembly fitting to the can. Optional: Drill a small hole in the can just behind the N-type connector. Rain or condensation which finds its way into the can has an easy route out. The hole should not affect the performance of the cantenna.

Step Four
Attach the N-Male end of a pigtail (pictured below is a 60 inch MC-Card to N-Male LMR100 Type cable) to the N-Female panel mount connector on the can and the other end of the pigtail to your nic (wireless network card). Ready-made pigtails are available from the advertisers on this site. Important: Unless you already have a wireless networking card with an existing jack for an external antenna, you will need to either modify your particular card by taking it apart and modifying it with delicate, skilled soldering to attach an antenna jack (voiding your warranty), or consider buying a new/used card that already has a built-in jack.

Some common pigtails are:

MC Card to N-male for use with Orinoco, Proxim, Avaya wireless, Toshiba, Enterasys, Buffalo and others.
MMCX Plug (male) to N-male for use with Cisco, Samsung, Symbol, Zcomax, 3Com and

others.
RP-SMA Plug (female) to N-male for use with Linksys, Dlink, US Robotics, Zcomax, Zoomair and others.
RP-TNC Plug (female) to N-male for use with Cisco, Linksys, SMC, US Robotics and others.

Finish
When aiming the cantenna, the polarization is important. Polarization refers to whether the driven element inside is pointing skywards (vertical) or sideways (horizontal). The direction of the driven element should match the antenna it is communicating with. In other words, the plane of polarization is the same as the N-connector's that the "pigtail" cable connects to. Some users rotate their antenna at a 45 angle, giving it a mixed or split polarization. This might work better because the target antenna may not be on the same absolute plane as your antenna's mounting plane. A tripod is handy for mounting an antenna.

It's a probably a good idea to always point a cantenna away from you, even thought the power output is relatively low. Remember the can is a focused microwave device. More about health concerns here.

That's all there is to achieve a 10db or better gain at 2.4GHz. The coffee can design is simpler and easier to make than the pringles cantenna. Use either a high-quality female bulkhead (round) Type-N connector or a chassis/panel (square) Type-N connector. For an additional 5dB of gain use hardware cloth available at a hardware store to form a funnel 4"/102mm at the throat and 16"/406mm at the diameter with a length of 23"/584mm. Solder or epoxy it to the open end of the coffee can.

Note: They talk about N Connectors but I found that at my local electronics store, they had a better selection of BNC Connector parts, so I used BNC.

A WIFI Cantenna

Us a metal can (or two cans soldered together) and cut a rectangle hole in the bottom about 60mm from the bottom of the can.

Fit in can a 3G USB Modem or USB Aerial Adaptor.
Connect to your laptop.
Point the cantenna towards the nearest WIFI Signal..

Yet Another Cantenna

You need;
Large Steel can (top opened, emptied and cleaned)
Some Aluminium Foil
Some Packaging Tape

Perhaps some cardboard to mount the foil on.

Cut some Aluminium Foil and mount on top of can and around behind cellphone.
Do not put cellphone in the centre but experiment in the cellphones location on the can and also the location of the can.
Good for a Cell Phone or a WIFI Aerial Booster.

Cat Box
I used some scrap ply to make a cat box. The lid pulls off so I can put some food and water into the box and maybe leave the cat for several days.

The box measures 500mm wide, 500mm high and 500mm deep.

It will get a coat of paint and a nice blanket and a couple of food tins inside and my cat will be happy.

The lid lifts off so you have access to the inside of the box.

Compost Bin

I dismantled an old laundry washing machine to use for a compost bin.

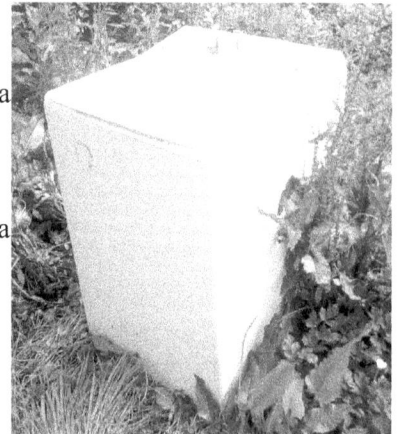

I am using the case of the machine by just plonking it on a spot, fill it then move it and start again.

Garden Boxes

I used some old timber to make some garden and potato boxes.

150x25mm roughly 1200mm long and 600mm wide.

Just a couple will make enough vegetables for 1-2 people.

You simply place on the ground. Place in plenty of newspaper to suppress the weeds. Put in some manure and compost and plant some seeds or plants.

Herb Garden

I used the internal part of the laundry washing machine and will make a herb garden out of it.

Hot/Cold Box

I used some surplus polystyrene (100mm or 4 inches thick) and some tape to make a hot or cold box.

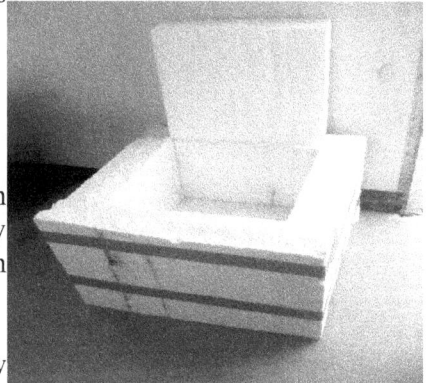

You could use hay etc. as well.

The idea is to cook a casserole or a stew as normal on an element or gas ring in a pot or dish. When it is thoroughly hot maybe after 15-20 minutes, take the pot and place it in the hot box an cover.

The cooking will continue for many hours. Just a slow cooker fundamentally.

You could line and put an outer on the box to make it more airtight.

Storage Containers

I used some old plastic milk bottles to cut and make into nail, screw, food, etc. containers.

Easy and Cheap.

Outdoor Table

I plan to build an outdoor picnic table like the one in this plan.

Mine is 1200mm long. Enough to seat four people.

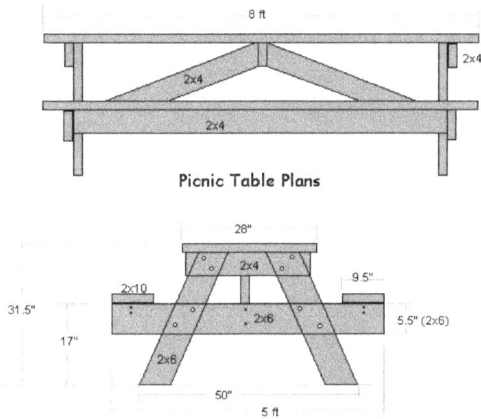

Picnic Table Plans

Home Made Rocket Stove

http://www.off-grid.net/tag/rocket-stove/

Simple to make from a plastic bucket, some coke bottles and some adobe/cob using dirt, grass (or hay or straw) and water.

DIY washing machine

What do you get when you combine a 5 gallon bucket and a toilet plunger? An off grid washing machine. Well, maybe not a machine in the traditional sense, unless you consider my hands the motor. This is something I have been wanting to make for quite some time now. The other day while I was in town, I saw a toilet plunger on the shelf and put it in my cart.

This primitive prototype washing machine started out as a 5 gallon bucket and the plunger. I handed the plunger to PB and asked him to cut some holes in the plunger, that makes it easier to plunge the clothes without making tons of bubbles and a big mess. I left it up to PB to decide how to cut the holes and in what shape. He took it downstairs for a few minutes, then brought it back to me, he handed me the plunger with 3, perfectly round, quarter sized holes. he handed me the rubber plugs that came from those centres.

Plunger with holes

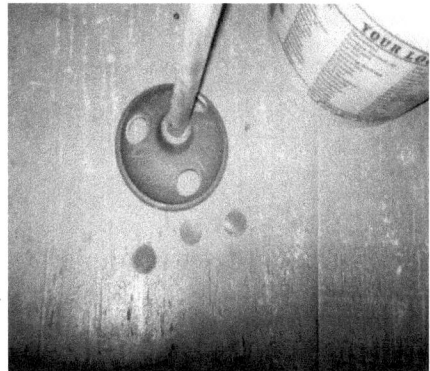

http://www.off-grid.net/2010/04/22/diy-washing-machine-and-homemade-laundry-soap/

Light a Fire with Coke Can and Toothpaste

The idea behind starting a fire with a coke can and toothpaste is that one day you might find yourself stranded somewhere with limited resources. Coke cans are pretty common, and I can definitely imagine a scenario where your cruise ship is sunk in the Aegean Sea and the only materials you have were in the polystyrene cooler you dragged ashore.

The toothpaste is a gentle abrasive. Sand is also an abrasive, but sand would probably leave bigger scratches than the ones it was smoothing. You can also use chocolate to polish the can.

Simply polish the bottom of the can for a few minutes and get it really shiny. Then use a twig of a piece of paper and hold up to the sun, find the focal point of the can and after a few minutes you will have fire!

Mini-Glass House

My Mini-Glass House is 500mm wide, 500mm long and 400mm high. It is made of scrap ply and polycarbonate.

My Dream House

I would love to build a nice small house, possible a double garage made into a small one bedroom home.

6m x 4.2m is a nice size.

Habitable Home Plan
Bill Rosoman
1425 Rotowaro Road, Glen afton

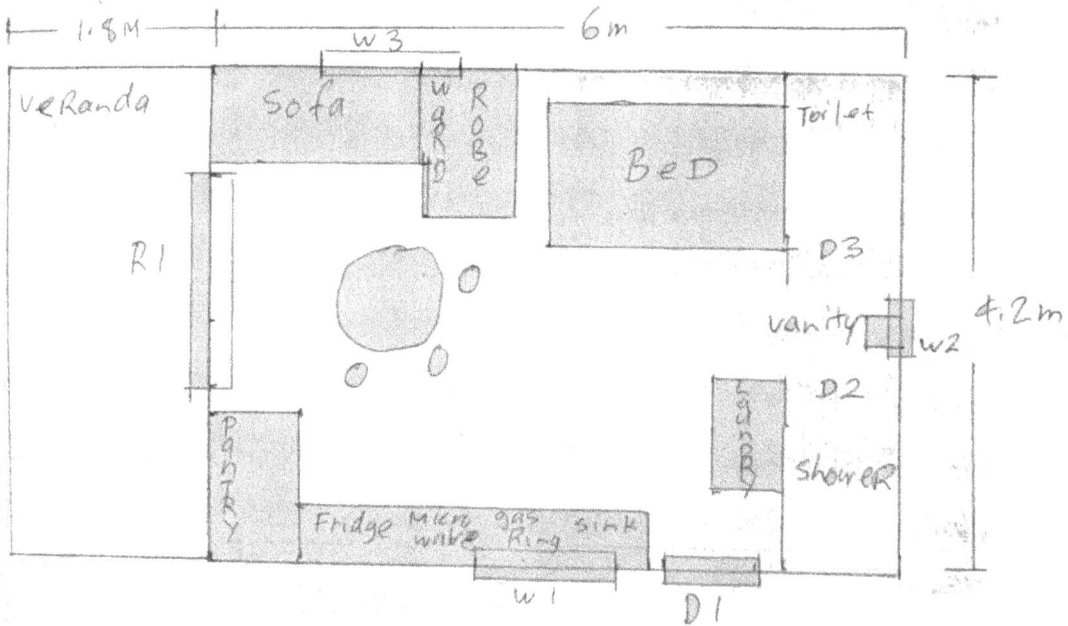

Well that was the dream, but the reality is that a one bedroom cottage would cost $60-65,000.00.

So plan B is to look at two 6m containers as a home. The Shell cost of around $15,000 and then internal stuff like walls and doors and also external like plumbing and waste water etc.

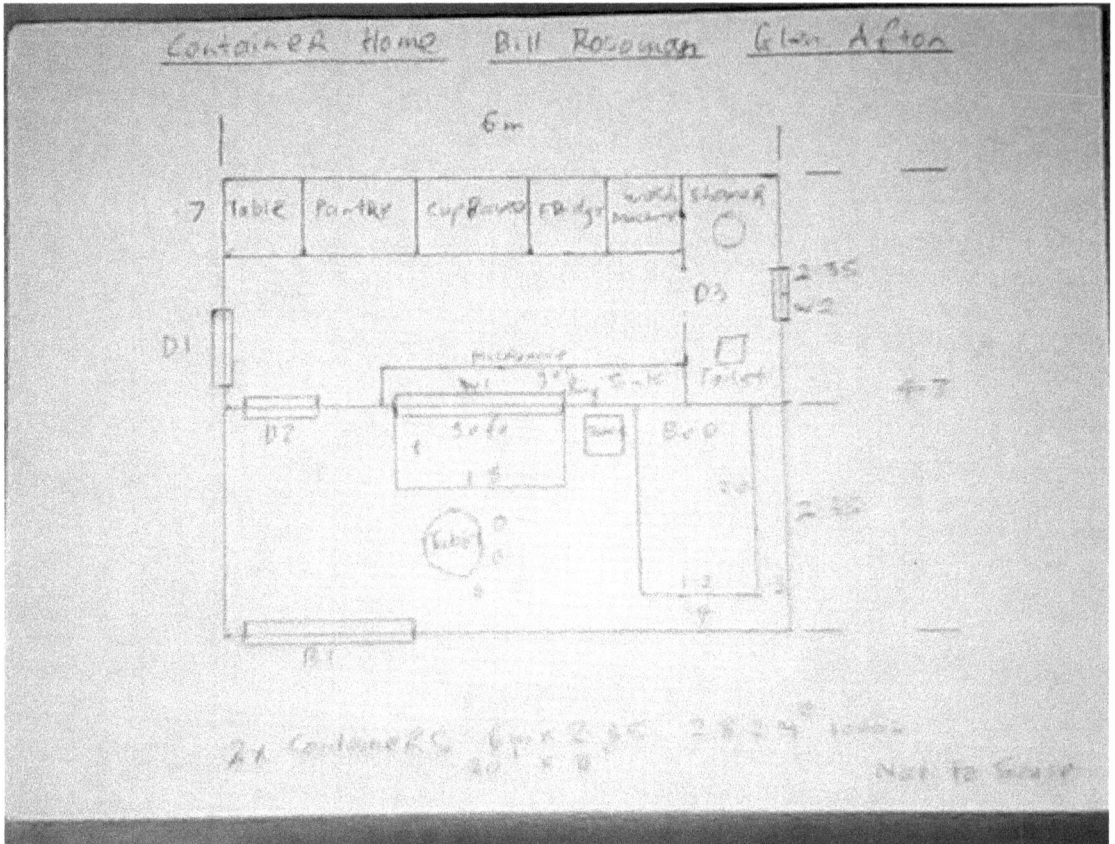

Container Home   Bill Rosoman   Glen Afton

Building a New Home

I built my own home in 1979 and it is still standing. It was a kitset home and I did most of the work, except the plumbing and drain laying.

In those days there was not much red tape and as it was a small rural area I was able to work well with the Building Inspector, The District Engineer and the Health Inspector (he was a little bit of a problem, but we got there).

However nowadays there seems to be so much red tape it is mind boggling. Also there are costs to everything.

Building consent
Plans and Specifications
Applicants Check list
You have 12 months to start a project and two years to complete it.

They require a mountain of paperwork and you have little choice but to do it.

I have worked out the cost for a one bedroom home of 42m2 at around $60,000

I need
Smoke alarm x 2
Compost toilet
Grey water soakage system
water tank
house (shell only)
retaining walls x 2
prepare building site
LPG double gas ring stove
LPG hot water callifont
LPG Heater
9kg LPG bottles x 2
Permits and Consents
Cut Trees
Solar panels x 2
Solar battery and controller
Plumber
Drainlayer
Gib wall Fixer
Landscaper for retaining walls
Timber and fittings
Pipes and fittings
Electrical wire and fittings
230v Inverter 2000w

I will do most of the internal work and all the electrical work, as it is mostly 12 volts and not connected to the mains power.

Applicant's Checklist:

Dwellings
Project examples: New dwellings, dwelling alterations and/or additions, change of building use to habitable

Applicants Name: Project Location:

Only completed Applications can be accepted for lodgement.

Key: tick = Provided X = Not Provided l I or -- = Not Applicable

PLEASE FILL IN
OFFICE USE ONLY

COMPLETE ALL SECTIONS OF THE APPLICATION FORM

All sections of the application form have been completed.

A copy of the FULL Certificate of Title (up to 2 months old).

Good quality drawings to an appropriate scale of 1:100 (detail 1:50, site plan 1:200) with metric dimensions.

Please provide 2 copies of all plans and specifications. (Please note Hamilton City Council & Matamata-Piako District Council require 3 sets of plans and specifications).

Deposit Fee.

SITE PLAN
Show the legal boundaries of the site, and easements. Show the location and distances of all existing and proposed buildings, including accessory buildings such as sheds or garages, in relation to the boundaries. Use an appropriate metric scale of 1:200 or 1:100 and include a north point.

Show the layout of existing and proposed sanitary and stormwater drains. Include the location of each drain's connection to the public mains. Provide details of on-site stormwater disposal, e.g. rain tanks, soak holes etc. (Check that kerb connection is acceptable if the site is unsuitable for on-site disposal or a Council stormwater connection is unavailable.) Where a septic tank is used include details of the size and location of tank and of the effluent field and calculations.

Indicate the top of any banks shown and their gradient contours in relation to the building. Show the height of the bank and the distance from the top of the bank to the building.

A geotechnical report from an appropriately qualified person may be required.

If the title is less than five hectares, show the gross floor area of all buildings on the title.

Show the dimensions of any existing and/or proposed vehicle entranceway and its position along the boundary. For a new entranceway, include a completed application form for a new entrance/crossing.

If the property is in an urban area, show car parking and vehicle circulation provisions, including on-site manoeuvring. Mark the street names on the site plan.

Swimming / Spa Pools (if applicable) – requirement of Applicant Checklist for Pools have been met.

FLOOR PLANS

Supply a floor plan of each level, including complete floor layout and use of each area. Floor areas and roof areas in square metres should be shown on plans drawn to an appropriate scale, e.g. 1:100 or 1:50. Show the location of all plumbing fittings and all waste and vent pipes.

Show location and size of windows and doors.

Show location of smoke alarms.

Heaters/Solar Systems (if applicable): Requirements of the Applicant Checklist for Heaters/Solar Systems have been met.

ELEVATION PLAN

Supply an elevation plan of each external wall showing heights from eaves to finished ground level at each external corner, and the existing and proposed land contours. Also show the overall height of the building from ground level to the apex of the roof.

Show type of cladding.

Show location of wall and roof bracing and of all opening window sashes.

Show window size and type of glazing.

FOUNDATION PLAN

For timber floors show the location of piles, pile type, sub floor bracing, foundation perimeter walls and internal piling system where applicable.

Provide sub floor bracing calculations for timber floors.

For concrete floors provide clear CROSS-SECTION DETAILS and show location of slab thickenings and steel.

Attach specific foundation design. A structural engineer-designed foundation is required for buildings on weak soils, sloping sites and pole foundations over 3m high.

STRUCTURAL BRACING CALCULATIONS

Supply bracing calculations in an approved form. Show the location of the pile bracing elements and the wall bracing elements on the floor plan and the roof bracing on the truss plan. (For 1 - 2 room additions the location, type and value of the bracing element will be sufficient).

SPECIFIC CONSTRUCTION DETAILS - Please provide the following specific details where appropriate

Flashing details between roofs and walls.

Flashing and weathering details between upper floor decks and floors.

Fixings for ballustrading to decks.

Post/beam fixings.

Foundation details such as reinforcing size and location.

CROSS-SECTIONAL DETAILS
Provide sufficient scaled cross-section drawings (1:50 or better) through the building to show foundation details, floor systems, wall, ceiling and roof construction. A finalised roof truss/framing plan must be provided with the application.

Show construction details of terraces, steps, stairs (internal and external), barriers and balustrades.

Where the position of beams, supports and connections are not clear, these should be shown with details of connections at a scale of 1:50 or 1:20.

Show the location and type of wall cladding and roof sheathing. For composite systems, that are alternative solutions to the Building Code, these should be designated on the CROSS-SECTION plan and referenced in the SPECIFICATIONS.

Give details of thermal insulation: type and R. value. (For buildings with glazing less than 30% of wall area, use NZS 4218: Schedule method or the calculation or modelling methods. If the glazing area is more than 30% you can not use the schedule method.

Construction details included (e.g. flashings, cladding junctions, wall/soffit junctions etc.)

FIRE WALL AND FIRE RATING REQUIREMENTS
If using an approved and tested system, provide details and state the particular design type and number here: ....

If the system is specifically designed by an engineer, then supply the specific design.

PLUMBING

Specify AS/NZS 3500 or G13 plumbing system. Plan must show positions of all fittings and pipe sizes.

For multi-level residential housing provide isometric drawings of the plumbing reticulation including soil and waste system showing positions of all fittings and pipe sizing.

SPECIFICATIONS
The specification should be project specific and appropriate to the building construction. It should be laid out in easily followed sections covering methods and materials that are not included in the building plans, e.g. pipe work materials.

Include manufacturer's specifications of any solid fuel heater or solar system.

SPECIFIC DESIGN
If specific design is used, a structural engineer's Design Producer Statement (PS1), drawings and calculations must be supplied. A peer review may be required, provided by Council's engineering consultants at cost to the applicant.

An engineer's letter of supervision may be required.

Any buildings that fall outside the scope of NZS 3604:1.1.2 require specific design. Specific design is also required for structural steel frames, foundations on weak soils, large retaining walls and waste water disposal systems.

EFFLUENT DISPOSAL
If an on-site effluent disposal system ('septic tank') is required, provide plans for the system, including certification from a suitably qualified person, that the system is suitable for the site and complies with the regional and local rules for waste water disposal.

WEATHERTIGHTNESS
For all new dwellings and additions, or where alterations impact on the building envelop a weathertightness Risk Matrix Calculation must be provided – refer to NZ Building Code E2.AS1.3.0

WATER, WASTE WATER, STORMWATER CONNECTIONS
Provide a scaled site plan showing the location of any new stormwater, waste water and/or water connections.

If residential, show stormwater connections to kerb and channel on the site plan. If no Council stormwater services are available to the property, provide details of on-site disposal, e.g. soak holes.

Waste Water Connection
If no new waste water connection has been installed to service the new dwelling or

development, please apply for a connection and pay fees. (Provide site plan for approval).

If there are no waste water reticulation services available to the property, ensure that details of the size of the septic tank and of the effluent field are included on the site plan and with the specifications.

Water Connection
If no water connection been installed to service the new dwelling or development, please apply for a connection and submit with fees. (Provide site plan for approval).

Has an identifying marker been placed on the boundary where you require the water connection to be located?

If there are no Council water reticulation services available to the property, provide details of the source of the existing or proposed water supply.

APPLICANT'S DECLARATION: I have provided all the required information:

…………………………………………………… (Applicant) …………………… (Date)

OFFICE USE ONLY OUTCOME OF DECISIONS

 This application was accepted for lodgement because all required information was supplied

 This application was not accepted for lodgement because documentation was incomplete

 Documentation is now complete and the application is accepted for lodgement

 Officer…………………………………………… Date……………………

Jeez what a list of stuff you have to do!

Some Building Websites

www.buildwaikato.co.nz
www.waikatodc.govt.nz/Documents/Plans/District-plan/Proposed-district-plan.aspx
www.dbh.govt.nz/building-code-compliance-documents-downloads#G9
www.smarterhomes.org.nz/water/on-site-sewage-systems/
www.consumerbuild.org.nz/publish/buildact-consents.php
www.dbh.govt.nz/buildingactreview-exemptions
www.compostingtoilet.org
www.weathercity.com/nz/glen_afton/

www.facebook.com/pages/Glen-Afton-New-Zealand/110350228977861
www.motowhere.com/maps/route/Hamilton-Kiwibiker-Lines-Tips-Ride-Glen-Afton-Route
www.lifestyleblock.co.nz/index.php
www.rd1.com
www.facebook.com/pages/Free-Food-New-Zealand/118166358866
www.smarterhomes.org.nz
www.sustainability.govt.nz /
www.homestead.org
www.motherearthnews.com
www.permies.com/permaculture-forums
www.appropedia.org/Welcome_to_Appropedia
www.archive.org/
www.off-grid.net /
www.offgridsurvival.com
www.judyofthewoods.net/homestead.html
www.shtfplan.com/
www.livingonadime.com/
www.frugalkiwi.co.nz/

On the Road Information and Phone Numbers

On The Road Assistance/Information in New Zealand

Organisation	Comment	Phone	Website
101 Must do weekends	Travel		www.aatravel.co.nz/101
2 Degree Mobile	Phone Internet	0800-022-022	www.2degreesmobile.co.nz
AA	Motoring	0800-456-654	www.aa.co.nz
AA Insurance		0800-500-213	www.aainsurance.co.nz
AA Repairs	Vehicles	0800-456-654	www.aa.co.nz
AA Rescue	Breakdowns	0800-500-222	www.aa.co.nz
AA Travel		0800-500-543	www.aatravel.co.nz
ACC	Accidents	0800-101-996	www.acc.co.nz
Accommodation			www.aatravel.co.nz/accommodation-newzealand
Acer Computers		0800-223-769	www.acer.co.nz
Air NZ	Airline	0800 737 000	www.airnewzealand.co.nz
Ambulance	Non-Urgent	0800-426-285	
Animals	Ill Treatment	0800-008-333	www.maf.govt.nz
ANZ	Bank	0800-269-296	www.anz.co.nz
ASB Bank	Bank	0800-803-804	www.asb.co.nz
Babylon Communications	Electronic Install	0800-255-255	www.babylon.net.nz
Batteries Marshall		0800-800-779	www.marshallbatteries.co.nz
Batterymart	Batteries	0800-24-50-24	www.batterymart.co.nz
Beaurepaires	Tyres	0800-489-737	www.beaurepaires.co.nz
Bluebridge Ferry	Ferry N/S Island	0800-844-844	www.bluebridge.co.nz
BNZ	Bank	0800-800-468	www.bnz.co.nz
BP	Fuel Oil	0800-800-027	www.bp.co.nz
Bunnings Warehouse	Building Supplies	0508-286-646	www.bunnings.co.nz
Burnsco	Outdoors Equipment	0800-10-20-40	www.burnsco.co.nz
Caltex	Fuel	0800-733-835	www.caltex.co.nz
Caravan Parks	Caravan Parks		www.caravan-parkfinder.co.nz
Cheap Chat	Phone Card	0800-552-885	www.prepaidcards.co.nz/cheapchat.cfm
Cheap Living	Oily Rag		www.oilyrag.co.nz
Citizen Advice	Bureau	0800-367-222	www.cab.org.nz
Courier Post		0800-268-7437	www.courierpost.co.nz
Covi Insurance		0800-805-965	www.covi.co.nz
Creative Kiwis	Books Photos etc		www.creativekwis.com
Crime Stoppers		0800-555-111	www.crimestoppers-nz.org
Dick Smith Electronics	Electronic Retail	0800-373-347	www.dse.co.nz
DOC	Conservation	0800-362-468	www.doc.govt.nz
DOC	Conservation	0800 362 468	www.doc.govt.nz
Edmonds Cookbook	Cooking		www.nzete.org/tm/scholarly/tei-14mCookbook.html
Emergency	Police Fire Ambulance	111	www.111emergency.co.nz
Family Parks	Camp Grounds		www.familyparks.co.nz
Far North Fuels	Fuel Oil	0800-43-83-83	www.farnorthfuels.co.nz
Flight Centre	Travel	0800-35-44-48	www.flightcentre.co.nz
Free Library	Online Library		www.thefreelibrary.com
Genesis Energy		0800 300 400	www.genesisenergy.co.nz
Goodyear	Tyres	0800-657-596	www.goodyear.co.nz
Google Maps	Directions		www.Maps.Google.co.nz
Government	Helpline	0800-779-997	www.newzealand.govt.nz
Hamilton Mechanic	Mobile	0800-929-213	
Harvey Norman	Electronic Retail	0508-46-42-78	www.harveynorman.co.nz
Healthline	Health Advice	0800-611-116	www.moh.govt.nz/healthline
Holiday Parks	Camp Grounds		www.hapnz.co.nz
House of Travel		0800-739-009	www.houseoftravel.co.nz
Ink Post	Printer Ink	0800-465-767	www.inkpost.co.nz
Interislander	Ferry N/S Island	0800-802-802	www.interislander.co.nz
ITM	Building Supplies	0800-367-486	www.itm.co.nz
Kidsline		0800-543-754	www.kidsline.org.nz
Kiwi Bank		0800-11-33-55	www.kiwibank.co.nz
Kiwi Holiday Parks	Holiday Parks		www.kiwiholidayparks.com
Land Transport		0800 822 422	www.nzta.govt.nz
Language Line		0800-108-809	
Latest highway conditions			www.nzta.govt.nz/traffic/current-conditions/highway-info/index.html
Live traffic webcams			www.nzta.govt.nz/traffic/current-conditions/webcams/index.html
Lonely Planet	New Zealand		www.lonelyplanet.com/new-zealand
Mental Health	Emergencies	0800-50-50-50	
Mobil	Fuel Oil	0800-808-666	www.mobil.co.nz
Need A Nerd	Computers	0800-63-33-26	www.needanerd.co.nz
News Talk ZB	Radio	0800-801-080	www.newstalkzb.co.nz
Next Electronics	Electronic Repairs	0800-466-398	www.nextelectronics.co.nz
NZ Camping	Camp Grounds		www.nzcamping.co.nz
NZ Courier		0800-800-841	www.nzcouriers.co.nz
NZ Post		0800-501-501	www.nzpost.co.nz
NZ Transport Agency	Breakdowns	0800-108-809	www.nzta.govt.nz
NZI Assist		0800-694-555	www.nzi.co.nz
NZInsurance		0800-694-222	www.nzi.co.nz
NZMCA	Association	09-298-5466	www.nzmca.org.nz
Ongas-LPG		0800-84-12-12	www.ongas.co.nz
Online Office	Mobile Office		www.webng.com/leftfieldnz/onlineoffice.html
Passport		0800-22-50-50	www.dia.govt.nz
Pests Disease	MAF Biosecurity	0800-809-966	www.maf.govt.nz
Pet Friendly	Camping		www.petsoncamp.co.nz
Photo Editing	Online Photo Editing		www.picnik.com
PickNZ	Seasonal Work	0800-742-569	www.picknz.co.nz
Poachers	MAF	0800-476-224	www.fish.govt.nz
Poisons Centre		0800-764-766	www.poisons.co.nz
Powerco	Energy	0800-27-27-27	www.powerco.co.nz
Powershop	Energy	0800-10-00-60	www.powershop.co.nz
Private Box	Mail Redirection	0800-122-335	www.privatebox.co.nz
Radio NZ	TXT 2101	0800-653-389	www.radionz.co.nz
Railway	Emergencies	0800-808-400	
Rape Crisis		0800-472-496	www.rapecrisis.org.nz
Red Cross		0800-733-276	www.redcross.org.nz
RV Supplies	RV Supplies	07-846-771	www.rvwholesalesupplies.co.nz
RV Worldstore	RV Supplies	03-541-0994	www.rvworldstore.co.nz
Samaritans	Personal Crisis	0800-726-666	www.samaritans.org.nz
Seasonal Work			www.seasonalwork.co.nz
Security ADT		0800-276-687	www.adtsecurity.co.nz
Shell Oil	Fuel Oil	0800-474-355	www.shell.co.nz
Smart Marine	RV Supplies	0800-80-50-40	www.smartmarine.co.nz
Snow Reports	Skiing		www.snowreports.co.nz
SOS Hamilton	Tradesmen	0800-767-669	www.sosnow.co.nz
St John		0800-785-646	www.stjohn.org.nz
Supercharge	Batteries	0800-188-122	www.superchargebatteries.co.nz
TAB	Racing Betting	0800-10-20-33	www.tab.co.nz
Telecom	Phone Internet	0800-000-000	www.telecom.co.nz
Telecom Faults	Phone Internet	0800-800-123	www.telecom.co.nz
Time	Telecom	0800-000-000	
Tisco	Electronic Repairs	0800-277-277	www.tisco.net.nz
Translate			http://translate.google.com
Translate Maori			http://www.learningmedia.co.nz/ngata
Translation Service		0800-872-675	
Travel Maps			http://map.bluecastle.co.nz
Travel Planner			www.travelplanner.co.nz/maps
Trip Planner			www.nowwhere.com.au/bp/nzlocator/tripPlan.aspx
Vector Energy		0800-80-23-32	www.vector.co.nz
Vehicle Reg Check		0508-777-746	TXT reg'vin to 3463
Vodafone	Phone Internet	0800-800-021	www.vodafone.co.nz
Weather	Met Service		www.metservice.co.nz/national
Web Search	Information		www.google.co.nz
WINZ	Benefits	0800-559-009	www.workandincome.govt.nz
World Clock	Time		www.timeanddate.com/worldclock
YHA	Accommodation	0800-278-299	www.yha.co.nz
Youth Line		0800-4376-633	www.youthline.co.nz

All care taken, but no responsibility
Any updates additions to TXT 021-233-5427 Email leftfieldnz@gmail.com
Bill Rosoman 2010   *Some 0800 numbers maybe not available from a Cell Phone*

The Future

In a little while I will be 65 years old. At that time I will start receiving New Zealand Superannuation and a Gold Card which gives special privileges like free buses out of peak hours. I will also have the funds from my Compulsory Savings Account, Kiwisaver which will be around $15,000.

At that time I will decide about building a home or perhaps a double garage to live in.

In the meantime I will live in my mobile home and the container.

So my new life is a work in progress, but at least it will keep me busy and I will have plenty of things to do in my old age LOL.

Conclusion

After writing this book and cruising online I realise that it is impossible to be totally self-sufficient and to live in isolation.

I will be doing what I can to cut costs and to live a simple and cheap life in the country.

I will enjoy myself tending the garden or doing some hobbies or making things to make life a little easier.

I will update the book as I go along.

It has been very interesting seeing what people are thinking about and how some are getting prepared in case TSHTF and most people seem to just cruise along with their 9 till 5 job paying the mortgage and hoping nothing happens to shatter their world.

I guess I am somewhere in the middle, I like to live the simple life and to do it cheaply and I enjoy doing things for myself. I also believe that one should be a little prepared in case something may happen to your world, were things turn to custard and normal situations of shops and services etc. are disrupted.

So I am making my property liveable and I am stocking up on food and provisions.

I will make quite a few things to make life easier and then relax and enjoy the fruits of my labour, literally.

So I reckon it will not hurt if you read books like this and maybe get cracking with some extra supplies and some plans, just in case TSHTF.

"Every day, think as you wake up, today I am fortunate to be alive, I have a precious human life, I am not going to waste it. I am going to use all my energies to develop myself, to expand my heart out to others; to achieve enlightenment for the benefit of all beings. I am going to have kind thoughts towards others, I am not going to get angry or think badly about others. I am going to benefit others as much as I can."
— Dalai Lama XIV

Have fun and do not take life to seriously, but remember this is not a dress rehearsal. LOL.

OUTBACK BAROMETER

Place String Here -------------------->

If String Wet It's Raining

If String Dry it's Not Raining

If String Swaying it's Windy

If String Stands Sideways it's Very Windy

If String Casts No Shadow it's Cloudy

If String Stiff it's Freezing
   (check Brass Monkey)

If String Invisible it's Night Time

If String Not Stiff it's Warm

If String Smoking Place is On Fire

If String Hot There is a Drought

If String is Missing Natives are Restless

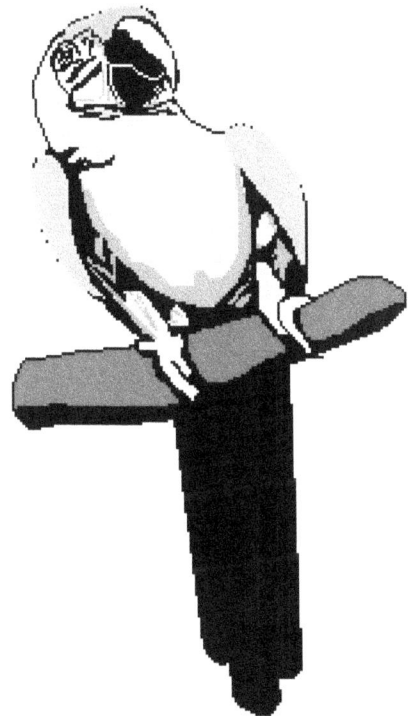

Other Books that may interest you

Craig Lock Books
https://www.smashwords.com/profile/view/craiglock

Ebooks
http://stores.lulu.com/craiglock

Bill Rosoman Books
http://stores.lulu.com/leftfieldnz

Ebooks
https://www.smashwords.com/profile/view/leftfieldnz

Our Main Website
http://www.creativekiwis.com

Bill Rosoman Books/Ebooks

The Ultimate Desktop Publishing Book

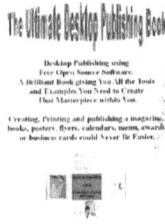

Desktop Publishing using Free Open Source Software. A Brilliant Book giving You

All the Tools and Examples You Need to Create That Masterpiece within You. Creating and publishing a magazine, books, posters, flyers, calendar, menu, award certificates, or business cards could Never Be Easier. Using Free Open Source Software FOSS. Scribus, Open Office, Gimp, Inkscape, Calibre. By Bill Rosoman Dip CS

http://www.lulu.com/product/paperback/the-ultimate-desktop-publishing-book/14847923

The Simple On The Road Cook Book

The Simple On The Road Cook Book. A Useful Easy, Simple and Budget Conscious Guide for Bachelors and other Food Preparation and Cooking Challenged People. Especially if Living in a Confined Space or On The Road.

http://www.lulu.com/content/paperback-book/the-simple-on-the-road-cook-book/8674457

Howto for Windows and Internet Virgins (book)

A Howto for Windows and Internet Virgins using the Windows Operating System. A Beginners Guide to using Window

http://www.lulu.com/content/paperback-book/howto-for-windows-and-internet-virgins/6121427

Te Ao Wiremu, Bill's World

Te Ao Wiremu, Bill's World, Honorary Black, Thirty years on the East Coast. Bill Rosoman spent 29 years living and working on the East Coast of the North Island of New Zealand above Gisborne. This is his yarn about his life there and the funny and not so funny things that happened.

http://www.lulu.com/content/paperback-book/te-ao-wiremu-bills-world/4030752

Get a Life (The Dummies Guide To Life)

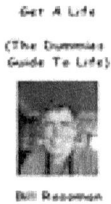

The book "Get a Life (The Dummies Guide To Life)", grew out of my brushes with life and my life long study of and fascination with human nature. I also had a bout of cancer in 2006. I find it interesting how people react to big events like finding out you have cancer. Personally I believe you have to take the good with the bad and get on with it. So I decided to write my thoughts down on my laptop and see what comes up! LOL The opinions expressed are mostly my own with help from quotations etc.

http://www.lulu.com/content/paperback-book/get-a-life-%28the-dummies-guide-to-life%29/1262704
http://www.smashwords.com/books/view/31925

Android Tablet Apads How to

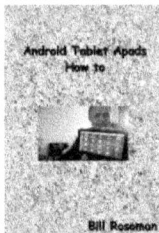

Android Tablets Apad How to", Some great Information for the use of Android Tablets. Tablets are the device of the future.

http://www.smashwords.com/books/view/35819

EPUB, How To Write and Publish an Ebook

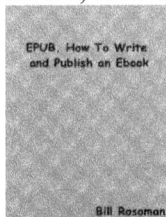

An ebook, "EPUB, How To Write and Publish an Ebook", using free software (FOSS), Writing and publishing and ebook is quite different from a hard copy book. This ebook gives you all the basic software and knowledge and skills to create your own epics for the modern age.

http://www.smashwords.com/books/view/32052

Puppy Linux Manual

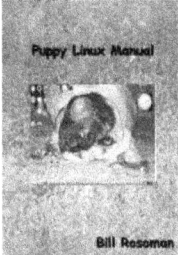

An ebook, "Puppy Linux Manual", Some great Information for the use of Puppy Linux, a Free Operating System which is great on older computers. Puppy Linux is also good for formatting and partitioning hard drives and rescuing data from crash computers.

http://www.smashwords.com/books/view/35818

Bill's Tome

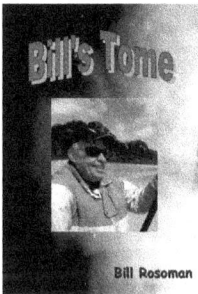

An ebook, "Bill's Tome", All That I Know Life, the Universe, Mortality etc.!

https://www.smashwords.com/books/view/41385

Creative Kiwis, an Amazing Journey

Bill Rosoman and Craig Lock

An ebook, "Creative Kiwis, an Amazing Journey", this book is about the journey of two people in the world of the Internet and Ebook and Book Publishing and Marketing. A massive journey and learning process.

http://www.smashwords.com/books/view/43270

A'holes That I've Known

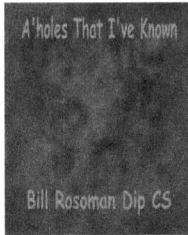

A look at some of the A'holes I have meet in my life. Life is not always a bed of roses and you have to deal with some not so nice people. Still life is great and you move through life and it's ups and downs. Being confident, articulate and assertive is the way to go, no door mouse for me. LOL

http://www.smashwords.com/books/view/44346
http://www.lulu.com/product/paperback/aholes-that-ive-known/14963987

Craig Lock Books/Ebooks

A New Dawn

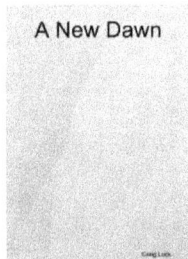

A passionate story of inspiration: hope, faith, peace and especially LOVE for the world and inspired by what I simply term God, the Creative Source of Life itself. That is my legacy to my beloved family...and the world. "But they that wait upon the Lord shall renew their strength, they shall mount up with wings as eagles; they shall run and not be weary; and they shall walk, and not faint." - Isiah 40:31

http://www.lulu.com/product/paperback/a-new-dawn/13399980
https://www.smashwords.com/books/view/42372

RETURN OF THE CHICKENS (e-book)

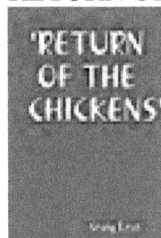

After that little interlude, I hope every one of you, the "New Safs" enjoy my book....and I hope you don't lynch me when you find me (like Salmon Rushdie) - something fishy going on? Because I believe that a sense of humour definitely helps in the hard but exciting years ahead of living in our "new beloved country".

http://www.lulu.com/content/e-book/return-of-the-chickens/9515900

Quote Unquote": Quotations that I like... very much (book)

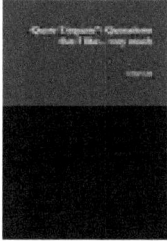

This is one of my first manuscripts and a rather short one at that - just like the author. I have also included a separate section on motivational quotes for all salespeople and on business in general (see Part Two). These often helped me in my rather more formal previous commercial career. But even if you are not in business , nor in sales you might find them inspiring (or inspirational) as we journey through the game that is life. I do. ... so time to get right into it / them and get "cracking" or "weaving" as my dear mother would say.

http://www.lulu.com/content/paperback-book/quote-unquote%e2%80%9d-quotations-that-i-like-very-much/9508150

Peace Lives Within (e-book)

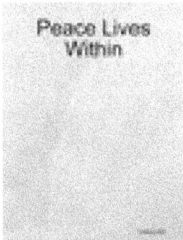

These are some notes that I've made recently (from my "red book"), which is forming the basis, the frame-work, the building-blocks for a new manuscript I'm writing. So will share with you and post extracts (hopefully regularly) on my Wordpress blog (craiglock.wordpress.com) as I write it. Hopefully I'll continue getting my "daily dose of inspiration".

https://www.smashwords.com/books/view/43299
http://www.lulu.com/content/e-book/peace-lives-within/9419604

To The End Of The Rainbow (e-book)

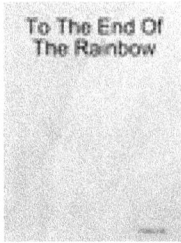

Craig has a 'passion' for writing books that tell stories about people doing positive things in this often so hard, sometimes unkind world, occasionally so cruel, yet always amazing world He loves 'telling tales', sharing true stories that leave the reader feeling uplifted, empowered and perhaps hopefully even inspired. Craig loves to try to "test his writing limits and imagination"and is currently writing 'To The End of the Rainbow'. I don't know how my story will end, but I do know how it all began!

http://www.lulu.com/content/e-book/to-the-end-of-the-rainbow/9419597

Angolan Dawn (book)

A true tale of an Angolan migrant miner who goes to 'e'Goli', the big city of gold in South Africa. Also a realistic portrayal of the Angolan conflict in "darkest Africa" through the eyes of a hospital orderly. A moving and realistic novel about the evil and destructiveness of war, as well as the inherent goodness within every human spirit. History, Angola, Southern Africa, Legacy, Gisborne, New Zealand, South Africa, Travel, Africa, War, Politics, Humanity, Conflict, Novel

http://www.lulu.com/content/paperback-book/angolan-dawn/8391177

How to Write a Book and Get Published (book)

Get Cracking and get your book written, completed and published now! We offer the complete package of helping you write that book within you and to get it published. At the end of the book you will have a published book, if you have a manuscript ready to go!

http://www.lulu.com/content/paperback-book/how-to-write-a-book-and-get-published/7313395

The New Rainbow (book)

THE NEW RAINBOW A tale of the many people in the rainbow nation of New South Africans

http://www.lulu.com/content/paperback-book/the-new-rainbow/7074514

I'LL DO IT MY WAY (book)

Childhood in South Africa, South African Politics and Apartheid and our new life in New Zealand

http://www.lulu.com/content/paperback-book/ill-do-it-my-way/6121816

Handbook for Survival in the Nineties and especially the New Millennium (book)

A collection of writings on various subjects to help every man or woman survive in a rapidly changing, uncertain world... after the "easy living and prosperity" of the seventies and eighties. An introductory look at the concepts of success, motivation, attitude, goal setting and stress

https://www.smashwords.com/books/view/43289
http://www.lulu.com/content/paperback-book/handbook-for-survival-in-the-nineties-and-especially-the-new-millenium/1660924

The End of the Line (book)

This is Craig Lock's first novel. A short novel set in "the beloved country". A passionate and heart-breaking tale of South Africa, a true story of the bad old days, but with the hope of the new. "The End Of The Line" could be described as a "faction", a fiction with a serious factual grounding. It is simple, and therefore moving. It gives yet another highly individual portrait of that troubled land, and it does so through a believable and sustained narrative form."

http://www.lulu.com/content/paperback-book/the-end-of-the-line/1630869
https://www.smashwords.com/books/view/42710

Dropped out In Godzone (book)

A new immigrant's impressions of life in provincial New Zealand (after coming from a large city in South Africa) ... and there were one or two rather funny adventures, nay escapades in "Sleepy Hollow" from time to time.

http://www.lulu.com/content/paperback-book/the-end-of-the-line/1630869
https://www.smashwords.com/books/view/42699

Over The Rainbow (book)

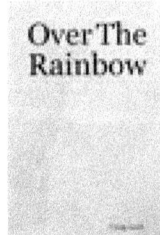

A look at the many colourful peoples, who make up this diverse and vibrant society, as seen through the eyes of a newspaper reporter. Many colourful "vignettes" in this "land of great contrasts" - happy, sad and true, that was the fabric of South African life in the lead up to the historic Democratic Election of 1994. We live in a very complex country of great disparities and extremes, especially in wealth and in living standards. A land of great contradictions: a land of sunshine, a world in one country, a land of laughter in this strange and beautiful place. Much of the laughter from the very people, who have suffered the most and felt the most pain in this strange tormented place of ours. Yes, there is that sadness in the eyes of them too. So to put it simply, South Africa is just one happy, sad land...and I hope that the lives of ALL South Africans will become better in the days ahead.

http://www.lulu.com/content/paperback-book/over-the-rainbow/1265824

Here There and Everywhere

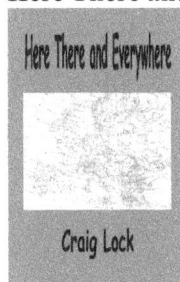

Craig Lock is an extensive world traveller and failed professional emigrater who has spent most of his life's savings on airfares. He is still 'sliding down the razor blade of life', stuck on a deserted (other than a few brilliant rugby players) island at the bottom of the world near Antarctica, where he is 'trying to throw a double six' to get off and go out into the real world - but he doesn't know where! In the style of Bill Bryson, HERE, THERE AND EVERYWHERE tells tales of His hilarious hair-raising adventures in his younger years through 'Grate' Britain and the Continent.

https://www.smashwords.com/books/view/44410
http://www.lulu.com/product/paperback/here-there-and-everywhere/15050656

Way Outback
by **Bill Rosoman**

First Published 2011

Way Outback is a practical guide to going bush way out back in the 21st century as a matter of dropping out financially for self-sufficiency, survival and protection, especially if TSHTF. People do not plan to fail, they just fail to plan.

Keywords:
Life, Humanity, survival, TSHTF, planning, future, financial crisis, self-sufficiency, survival, protection, danger, flood, fire, hurricane, disaster, disaster planning, survival guide, environmental crisis

###

www.ingramcontent.com/pod-product-compliance
Lightning Source LLC
Chambersburg PA
CBHW081212020426
42331CB00012B/3005